Find Hope in God:

with 800 Bible Verses and Promises

Find Hope in God: with 800 Bible Verses and Promises

ISBN: 9798345336663

About this Book

Are you trying to find lasting hope in this hopeless world?

The Bible says there is none in this world. This world is filled with suffering, tears, sins, crimes, bloodshed, tragedies, wars, injustice, poverty, anxiety, and countless more, and they are only increasing as we speak.

In the meantime, we humans all get older and eventually die and leave this world. So, there is no room for lasting hope in this world.

And everything you see—even your own body—is temporary, not eternal, and will be gone forever—according to the Bible.

The Bible, the Word of God, says there is lasting hope in God who made you and loves you. And he wants you to have eternal hope in him because he lives in Heaven forever.

But it's up to each person to choose where to go after they leave this temporary world. And God who doesn't force us gives us the freedom to choose.

So, you decide where to go after you leave this world.

Here is the Offer of lasting hope by God who loves you—He will erase all your troubles and sorrows and all their memories to heal you forever, and give you a brand-new, eternal body like Jesus to live with Him in Heaven forever in perfect peace and joy.

All you have to do is take the offer by believing in God through His Son Jesus! It's all free if you accept it by faith! Just confess your sins to God and accept His Eternal Salvation by believing in His Son Jesus who is the Savior of the world and the Giver of eternal hope. And follow Him all the way to Heaven.

This book has over 800 Bible verses and promises (You don't have to read them all) and it will help you know what the eternal hope is and how to get it.

This book is basically the same thing as my other book, "All You See Is Temporary," but was slightly modified for a different purpose.

Here is what the Bible says:

7 For we brought nothing into the world, and we certainly can't carry anything out.

1 Timothy 6:7

26 For what will it profit a man if he gains the whole world and forfeits his life?

Matthew 16:26

2 It is better to go to the house of mourning than to go to the house of feasting; for that is the end of all men, and the living should take this to heart.

Ecclesiastes 7:2

35 Jesus therefore said to them, ". . . He who walks in the darkness doesn't know where he is going. **36** While you have the light, believe in the light, that you may become children of light."

John 12:35–36

30 "Sirs, what must I do to be saved?" **31** They said, "Believe in the Lord Jesus Christ, and you will be saved . . ."

Acts 16:30-31

16 For God so loved the world, that he gave his one and only Son, that whoever believes in him should not perish, but have eternal life.

John 3:16

15 . . . The time is fulfilled, and God's Kingdom is at hand! Repent, and believe in the Good News.

Mark 1:15

9 . . . if you will confess with your mouth that Jesus is Lord, and believe in your heart that God raised him from the dead, you will be saved.

Romans 10:9

12 . . . for the same Lord is Lord of all, and is rich to all who call on him. **13** For, "Whoever will call on the name of the Lord will be saved."

Romans 10:12-13

24 Most certainly I tell you, he who hears my word and believes him who sent me has eternal life . . .

John 5:24

18 And the Lord will deliver me from every evil work, and will preserve me for his heavenly Kingdom. To him be the glory forever and ever. Amen.

2 Timothy 4:18

16 . . . because the former troubles are forgotten, and because they are hidden from my eyes. **17** For, behold, I create new heavens and a new earth; and the former things will not be remembered, nor come into mind.

Isaiah 65:16-17

4 He will wipe away every tear from their eyes. Death will be no more; neither will there be mourning, nor crying, nor pain, any more. The first things have passed away.

Revelation 21:4

13 But, according to his promise, we look for new heavens and a new earth, in which righteousness dwells.

2 Peter 3:13

All the glory goes back to God through Jesus!

So, enjoy and keep praising God!

Tadayoshi "Jacob" Minakawa
(October 15, 2024)

Special thanks to my wife for supporting me.

About the Translation

The World English Bible (WEB) comes in three versions: the American version (WEB), the British/Anglicized version (WEBBE), and the Messianic/Jewish Christian version (WMB). They are based on the American Standard Version of the Holy Bible which was published in 1901, and they update the archaic English of that version. They are in the public domain and are the only modern English translations of the Bible that are free of all copyright restrictions such as permission, permission fees, and permission expirations. That means you may copy, publish, proclaim, distribute, redistribute, sell, give away, quote, memorize, read publicly, broadcast, transmit, share, back up, post on the Internet, print, reproduce, preach, teach from, and use the World English Bible (WEB), the World English Bible British Edition (WEBBE), and the World Messianic Bible (WMB) as much as you want, and others may also do so. May God bless richly those involved in the great Work! They are good translations.

This book uses the World English Bible (WEB) for the New Testament verses, and the World English Bible British Edition (WEBBE) for the Old Testament verses. The WEB translates the word "the LORD" in the Old Testament as "Yahweh" as in "Yahweh is my shepherd" instead of "The LORD is my shepherd" (Psalm 23:1), whereas the WEBBE (British Edition) uses the word "the LORD" for the Old Testament. As for the New Testament, both the WEB and the WEBBE use the word "the LORD". Therefore, for the sake of consistency, I decided to use the WEBBE that uses the word "the LORD" for the Old Testament. Other smaller differences are in spelling and usage like "Savior" (WEB) and "Saviour" (WEBBE) and "among" (WEB) and "amongst" (WEBBE). Other than that, most of the verses quoted from both translations in this book are the same.

1. All You See Is Temporary

1. All People Die Eventually

21 Naked I came out of my mother's womb, and naked will I return there.

Job 1:21

27 Inasmuch as it is appointed for men to die once, and after this, judgment . . .

Hebrews 9:27

20 All go to one place. All are from the dust, and all turn to dust again.

Ecclesiastes 3:20

7 For we brought nothing into the world, and we certainly can't carry anything out.

1 Timothy 6:7

26 For what will it profit a man if he gains the whole world and forfeits his life?

Matthew 16:26

2 It is better to go to the house of mourning than to go to the house of feasting; for that is the end of all men, and the living should take this to heart.

Ecclesiastes 7:2

2. You Can Take Nothing with You

7 For we brought nothing into the world, and we certainly can't carry anything out.

1 Timothy 6:7

16 Don't be afraid when a man is made rich, when the glory of his house is increased; **17** for when he dies he will carry nothing away.

Psalm 49:16–17

21 Naked I came out of my mother's womb, and naked will I return there.

Job 1:21

26 For what will it profit a man if he gains the whole world and forfeits his life?

Matthew 16:26

19 Don't lay up treasures for yourselves on the earth, where moth and rust consume, and where thieves break through and steal . . .

Matthew 6:19

3. This World Will Be Gone Forever

7 But the heavens that exist now and the earth, by the same word have been stored up for fire, being reserved against the day of judgment and destruction of ungodly men.

2 Peter 3:7

1 I saw a new heaven and a new earth: for the first heaven and the first earth have passed away, and the sea is no more.

Revelation 21:1

8 The grass withers, the flower fades; but the word of our God stands forever.

Isaiah 40:8

35 Heaven and earth will pass away, but my words will not pass away.

Matthew 24:35

17 The world is passing away with its lusts, but he who does God's will remains forever.

1 John 2:17

4. This World Is Temporary

8 The grass withers, the flower fades; but the word of our God stands forever.

Isaiah 40:8

31 . . . For the mode of this world passes away.

1 Corinthians 7:31

16 For all that is in the world—the lust of the flesh, the lust of the eyes, and the pride of life—isn't the Father's, but is the world's. **17** The world is passing away with its lusts, but he who does God's will remains forever.

1 John 2:16–17

7 For we brought nothing into the world, and we certainly can't carry anything out.

1 Timothy 6:7

26 For what will it profit a man if he gains the whole world and forfeits his life?

Matthew 16:26

35 Heaven and earth will pass away, but my words will not pass away.

Matthew 24:35

17 The world is passing away with its lusts, but he who does God's will remains forever.

1 John 2:17

7 But the heavens that exist now and the earth, by the same word have been stored up for fire, being reserved against the day of judgment and destruction of ungodly men.

2 Peter 3:7

1 I saw a new heaven and a new earth: for the first heaven and the first earth have passed away, and the sea is no more.

Revelation 21:1

5. Even Your Own Body Is Temporary

63 It is the spirit who gives life. The flesh profits nothing. The words that I speak to you are spirit, and are life.

John 6:63

3 The LORD said, "My Spirit will not strive with man forever, because he also is flesh; so his days will be one hundred and twenty years."

Genesis 6:3

10 The days of our years are seventy, or even by reason of strength eighty years; yet their pride is but labour and sorrow, for it passes quickly, and we fly away.

Psalm 90:10

9 Don't reject me in my old age. Don't forsake me when my strength fails.

Psalm 71:9

4 LORD, show me my end, what is the measure of my days. Let me know how frail I am. **5** Behold, you have made my days hand widths. My lifetime is as nothing before you. Surely every man stands as a breath.

Psalm 39:4–5

47 Remember how short my time is, for what vanity you have created all the children of men!

Psalm 89:47

20 All go to one place. All are from the dust, and all turn to dust again.

Ecclesiastes 3:20

7 and the dust returns to the earth as it was, and the spirit returns to God who gave it.

Ecclesiastes 12:7

4 Man is like a breath. His days are like a shadow that passes away.

Psalm 144:4

50 Now I say this, brothers, that flesh and blood can't inherit God's Kingdom; neither does the perishable inherit imperishable.

1 Corinthians 15:50

3 For we are the circumcision, who worship God in the Spirit, and rejoice in Christ Jesus, and have no confidence in the flesh . . .

Philippians 3:3

21 Therefore let no one boast in men.

1 Corinthians 3:21

27 Inasmuch as it is appointed for men to die once, and after this, judgment . . .

Hebrews 9:27

1 For everything there is a season, and a time for every purpose under heaven: **2** a time to be born, and a time to die; a time to plant, and a time to pluck up that which is planted . . .

Ecclesiastes 3:1–2

1 A good name is better than fine perfume; and the day of death better than the day of one's birth. **2** It is better to go to the house of mourning than to go to the house of feasting; for that is the end of all men, and the living should take this to heart.

Ecclesiastes 7:1–2

6. All You See Is Temporary

8 The grass withers, the flower fades; but the word of our God stands forever.

Isaiah 40:8

9 Let the brother in humble circumstances glory in his high position; **10** and the rich, in that he is made humble, because like the flower in the grass, he will pass away.

James 1:9–10

16 For all that is in the world—the lust of the flesh, the lust of the eyes, and the pride of life—isn't the Father's, but is the world's. **17** The world is passing away with its lusts, but he who does God's will remains forever.

1 John 2:16–17

31 . . . For the mode of this world passes away.

1 Corinthians 7:31

7 For we brought nothing into the world, and we certainly can't carry anything out.

1 Timothy 6:7

26 For what will it profit a man if he gains the whole world and forfeits his life?

Matthew 16:26

35 Heaven and earth will pass away, but my words will not pass away.

Matthew 24:35

17 The world is passing away with its lusts, but he who does God's will remains forever.

1 John 2:17

7 But the heavens that exist now and the earth, by the same word have been stored up for fire, being reserved against the day of judgment and destruction of ungodly men.

2 Peter 3:7

1 I saw a new heaven and a new earth: for the first heaven and the first earth have passed away, and the sea is no more.

Revelation 21:1

2. There Is No True Hope in This World

1. This World Will Be Gone Forever

8 The grass withers, the flower fades; but the word of our God stands forever.

Isaiah 40:8

31 . . . For the mode of this world passes away.

1 Corinthians 7:31

35 Heaven and earth will pass away, but my words will not pass away.

Matthew 24:35

7 For we brought nothing into the world, and we certainly can't carry anything out.

1 Timothy 6:7

21 Naked I came out of my mother's womb, and naked will I return there.

Job 1:21

16 For all that is in the world—the lust of the flesh, the lust of the eyes, and the pride of life—isn't the Father's, but is the world's. **17** The world is passing away with its lusts, but he who does God's will remains forever.

1 John 2:16–17

7 But the heavens that exist now and the earth, by the same word have been stored up for fire, being reserved against the day of judgment and destruction of ungodly men.

2 Peter 3:7

1 I saw a new heaven and a new earth: for the first heaven and the first earth have passed away, and the sea is no more.

Revelation 21:1

2. What You See Is Not True Hope

24 . . . but hope that is seen is not hope. For who hopes for that which he sees?

Romans 8:24

16 For all that is in the world—the lust of the flesh, the lust of the eyes, and the pride of life—isn't the Father's, but is the world's. **17** The world is passing away with its lusts, but he who does God's will remains forever.

1 John 2:16–17

18 while we don't look at the things which are seen, but at the things which are not seen. For the things which are seen are temporal, but the things which are not seen are eternal.

2 Corinthians 4:18

3. What You See Is Not Your True Hope

24 . . . but hope that is seen is not hope. For who hopes for that which he sees?

Romans 8:24

16 For all that is in the world—the lust of the flesh, the lust of the eyes, and the pride of life—isn't the Father's, but is the world's. **17** The world is passing away with its lusts, but he who does God's will remains forever.

1 John 2:16–17

18 while we don't look at the things which are seen, but at the things which are not seen. For the things which are seen are temporal, but the things which are not seen are eternal.

2 Corinthians 4:18

22 Therefore you now have sorrow, but I will see you again, and your heart will rejoice, and no one will take your joy away from you.

John 16:22

4 He will wipe away every tear from their eyes. Death will be no more; neither will there be mourning, nor crying, nor pain, any more. The first things have passed away.

Revelation 21:4

20 . . . but rejoice that your names are written in heaven.

Luke 10:20

13 But, according to his promise, we look for new heavens and a new earth, in which righteousness dwells.

2 Peter 3:13

4. There Is No True Hope in This World

7 For we brought nothing into the world, and we certainly can't carry anything out.

1 Timothy 6:7

26 For what will it profit a man if he gains the whole world and forfeits his life?

Matthew 16:26

27 Inasmuch as it is appointed for men to die once, and after this, judgment . . .

Hebrews 9:27

20 All go to one place. All are from the dust, and all turn to dust again.

Ecclesiastes 3:20

24 . . . but hope that is seen is not hope. For who hopes for that which he sees?

Romans 8:24

18 . . . For the things which are seen are temporal, but the things which are not seen are eternal.

2 Corinthians 4:18

7 But the heavens that exist now and the earth, by the same word have been stored up for fire, being reserved against the day of judgment and destruction of ungodly men.

2 Peter 3:7

8 The grass withers, the flower fades; but the word of our God stands forever.

Isaiah 40:8

35 Heaven and earth will pass away, but my words will not pass away.

Matthew 24:35

17 The world is passing away with its lusts, but he who does God's will remains forever.

1 John 2:17

1 I saw a new heaven and a new earth: for the first heaven and the first earth have passed away, and the sea is no more.

Revelation 21:1

5. Why Do Good People Die?

1 The righteous perish, and no one lays it to heart. Merciful men are taken away, and no one considers that the righteous is taken away from the evil. **2** He enters into peace. They rest in their beds, each one who walks in his uprightness.

Isaiah 57:1–2

2 Therefore I praised the dead who have been long dead more than the living who are yet alive. **3** Yes, better than them both is him who has not yet been, who has not seen the evil work that is done under the sun.

Ecclesiastes 4:2–3

18 And the Lord will deliver me from every evil work, and will preserve me for his heavenly Kingdom. To him be the glory forever and ever. Amen.

2 Timothy 4:18

11 The counsel of the LORD stands fast forever, the thoughts of his heart to all generations.

Psalm 33:11

11 "For I know the thoughts that I think towards you," says the LORD, "thoughts of peace, and not of evil, to give you hope and a future."

Jeremiah 29:11

24 Father, I desire that they also whom you have given me be with me where I am, that they may see my glory, which you have given me, for you loved me before the foundation of the world.

John 17:24

28 If you loved me, you would have rejoiced, because I said "I am going to my Father;" for the Father is greater than I.

John 14:28

1 A good name is better than fine perfume; and the day of death better than the day of one's birth.

Ecclesiastes 7:1

15 Precious in the LORD's sight is the death of his saints.

Psalm 116:15

13 He will have pity on the poor and needy. He will save the souls of the needy. **14** He will redeem their soul from oppression and violence. Their blood will be precious in his sight.

Psalm 72:13–14

6 Therefore we are always confident and know that while we are at home in the body, we are absent from the Lord . . .

2 Corinthians 5:6

23 But I am hard pressed between the two, having the desire to depart and be with Christ, which is far better.

Philippians 1:23

8 We are courageous, I say, and are willing rather to be absent from the body and to be at home with the Lord.

2 Corinthians 5:8

21 For to me to live is Christ, and to die is gain.

Philippians 1:21

25 Jesus said to her, "I am the resurrection and the life. He who believes in me will still live, even if he dies."

John 11:25

11 This saying is trustworthy: "For if we died with him, we will also live with him. **12** If we endure, we will also reign with him."

2 Timothy 2:11-12

1 Don't let your heart be troubled. Believe in God. Believe also in me. **2** In my Father's house are many homes. If it weren't so, I would have told you. I am going to prepare a place for you. **3** If I go and prepare a place for you, I will come again, and will receive you to myself; that where I am, you may be there also.

John 14:1-3

3. There Is True Hope in God

1. There Is Lasting Hope in God

18 Indeed surely there is a future hope, and your hope will not be cut off.

Proverbs 23:18

1 For we know that if the earthly house of our tent is dissolved, we have a building from God, a house not made with hands, eternal, in the heavens.

2 Corinthians 5:1

13 But, according to his promise, we look for new heavens and a new earth, in which righteousness dwells.

2 Peter 3:13

18 And the Lord will deliver me from every evil work, and will preserve me for his heavenly Kingdom. To him be the glory forever and ever. Amen.

2 Timothy 4:18

16 . . . because the former troubles are forgotten, and because they are hidden from my eyes. **17** For, behold, I create new heavens and a new earth; and the former things will not be remembered, nor come into mind.

Isaiah 65:16-17

4 He will wipe away every tear from their eyes. Death will be no more; neither will there be mourning, nor crying, nor pain, any more. The first things have passed away.

Revelation 21:4

24 Most certainly I tell you, he who hears my word and believes him who sent me has eternal life, and doesn't come into judgment, but has passed out of death into life.

John 5:24

46 I have come as a light into the world, that whoever believes in me may not remain in the darkness.

John 12:46

12 Again, therefore, Jesus spoke to them, saying, "I am the light of the world. He who follows me will not walk in the darkness, but will have the light of life."

John 8:12

4 When Christ, our life, is revealed, then you will also be revealed with him in glory.

Colossians 3:4

42 So also is the resurrection of the dead. The body is sown perishable; it is raised imperishable. **43** It is sown in dishonor; it is raised in glory. It is sown in weakness; it is raised in power. **44** It is sown a natural body; it is raised a spiritual body. There is a natural body and there is also a spiritual body.

1 Corinthians 15:42-44

36 For they can't die any more, for they are like the angels, and are children of God, being children of the resurrection.

Luke 20:36

20 . . . but rejoice that your names are written in heaven.

Luke 10:20

20 For our citizenship is in heaven, from where we also wait for a Savior, the Lord Jesus Christ, **21** who will change the body of our humiliation to be conformed to the body of his glory . . .

Philippians 3:20-21

13 But now faith, hope, and love remain—these three. The greatest of these is love. **1** Follow after love . . .

1 Corinthians 13:13-14:1

2. True Hope of Eternal Heaven

16 . . . because the former troubles are forgotten, and because they are hidden from my eyes. **17** For, behold, I create new heavens and a new earth; and the former things will not be remembered, nor come into mind.

Isaiah 65:16-17

4 He will wipe away every tear from their eyes. Death will be no more; neither will there be mourning, nor crying, nor pain, any more. The first things have passed away.

Revelation 21:4

5 He who sits on the throne said, "Behold, I am making all things new." He said, "Write, for these words of God are faithful and true."

Revelation 21:5

4 When Christ, our life, is revealed, then you will also be revealed with him in glory.

Colossians 3:4

2 . . . we know that when he is revealed, we will be like him; for we will see him just as he is.

1 John 3:2

42 So also is the resurrection of the dead. The body is sown perishable; it is raised imperishable. **43** It is sown in dishonor; it is raised in glory. It is sown in weakness; it is raised in power. **44** It is sown a natural body; it is raised a spiritual body. There is a natural body and there is also a spiritual body.

1 Corinthians 15:42-44

36 For they can't die any more, for they are like the angels, and are children of God, being children of the resurrection.

Luke 20:36

9 It shall be said in that day, "Behold, this is our God! We have waited for him, and he will save us! This is the LORD! We have waited for him. We will be glad and rejoice in his salvation!"

Isaiah 25:9

17 . . . So we will be with the Lord forever.

1 Thessalonians 4:17

43 Jesus said to him, "Assuredly I tell you, today you will be with me in Paradise."

Luke 23:43

3 Those who are wise will shine as the brightness of the expanse. Those who turn many to righteousness will shine as the stars forever and ever.

Daniel 12:3

43 Then the righteous will shine like the sun in the Kingdom of their Father.

Matthew 13:43

3. No More Sorrow or Death

19 Many are the afflictions of the righteous, but the LORD delivers him out of them all.

Psalm 34:19

20 Your sun will not go down any more, nor will your moon withdraw itself; for the LORD will be your everlasting light, and the days of your mourning will end.

Isaiah 60:20

37 No, in all these things, we are more than conquerors through him who loved us.

Romans 8:37

57 But thanks be to God, who gives us the victory through our Lord Jesus Christ.

1 Corinthians 15:57

11 This saying is trustworthy: "For if we died with him, we will also live with him. **12** If we endure, we will also reign with him."

2 Timothy 2:11-12

25 Jesus said to her, "I am the resurrection and the life. He who believes in me will still live, even if he dies."

John 11:25

18 And the Lord will deliver me from every evil work, and will preserve me for his heavenly Kingdom. To him be the glory forever and ever. Amen.

2 Timothy 4:18

16 . . . because the former troubles are forgotten, and because they are hidden from my eyes. **17** For, behold, I create new heavens and a new earth; and the former things will not be remembered, nor come into mind.

Isaiah 65:16-17

4 He will wipe away every tear from their eyes. Death will be no more; neither will there be mourning, nor crying, nor pain, any more. The first things have passed away.

Revelation 21:4

28 so Christ also, having been offered once to bear the sins of many, will appear a second time, without sin, to those who are eagerly waiting for him for salvation.

Hebrews 9:28

20 For our citizenship is in heaven, from where we also wait for a Savior, the Lord Jesus Christ, **21** who will change the body of our humiliation to be conformed to the body of his glory . . .

Philippians 3:20-21

4 When Christ, our life, is revealed, then you will also be revealed with him in glory.

Colossians 3:4

2 . . . but we know that when he is revealed, we will be like him; for we will see him just as he is.

1 John 3:2

51 Behold, I tell you a mystery. We will not all sleep, but we will all be changed, **52** in a moment, in the twinkling of an eye, at the last trumpet. For the trumpet will sound and the dead will be raised incorruptible, and we will be changed.

1 Corinthians 15:51-52

42 So also is the resurrection of the dead. The body is sown perishable; it is raised imperishable. **43** It is sown in dishonor; it is raised in glory. It is sown in weakness; it is raised in power. **44** It is sown a natural body; it is raised a spiritual body. There is a natural body and there is also a spiritual body.

1 Corinthians 15:42-44

53 For this perishable body must become imperishable, and this mortal must put on immortality. **54** But when this perishable body will have become imperishable, and this mortal will have put on immortality, then what is written will happen: "Death is swallowed up in victory." **55** "Death, where is your sting? Hades, where is your victory?"

1 Corinthians 15:53-55

8 He has swallowed up death forever! The Lord GOD will wipe away tears from off all faces. He will take the reproach of his people away from off all the earth, for the LORD has spoken it. **9** It shall be said in that day, "Behold, this is our God! We have waited for him, and he will save us! This is the LORD! We have waited for him. We will be glad and rejoice in his salvation!"

Isaiah 25:8-9

35 But those who are considered worthy to attain to that age and the resurrection from the dead neither marry nor are given in marriage. **36** For they can't die any more, for they are like the angels, and are children of God, being children of the resurrection.

Luke 20:35-36

17 . . . So we will be with the Lord forever.

1 Thessalonians 4:17

43 Jesus said to him, "Assuredly I tell you, today you will be with me in Paradise."

Luke 23:43

3 Those who are wise will shine as the brightness of the expanse. Those who turn many to righteousness will shine as the stars forever and ever.

Daniel 12:3

43 Then the righteous will shine like the sun in the Kingdom of their Father.

Matthew 13:43

4. God Has a Whole New World for You!

1 I saw a new heaven and a new earth, for the first heaven and the first earth have passed away, and the sea is no more. **2** I saw the holy city, New Jerusalem, coming down out of heaven from God, prepared like a bride adorned for her husband.

Revelation 21:1–2

20 For our citizenship is in heaven, from where we also wait for a Savior, the Lord Jesus Christ, **21** who will change the body of our humiliation to be conformed to the body of his glory, according to the working by which he is able even to subject all things to himself.

Philippians 3:20-21

18 And the Lord will deliver me from every evil work, and will preserve me for his heavenly Kingdom. To him be the glory forever and ever. Amen.

2 Timothy 4:18

5 He who sits on the throne said, "Behold, I am making all things new."

Revelation 21:5

16 . . . because the former troubles are forgotten, and because they are hidden from my eyes. **17** For, behold, I create new heavens and a new earth; and the former things will not be remembered, nor come into mind.

Isaiah 65:16-17

4 He will wipe away every tear from their eyes. Death will be no more; neither will there be mourning, nor crying, nor pain, any more. The first things have passed away.

Revelation 21:4

18 But be glad and rejoice forever in that which I create; for, behold, I create Jerusalem to be a delight, and her people a joy. **19** I will rejoice in Jerusalem, and delight in my people; and the voice of weeping and the voice of crying will be heard in her no more.

Isaiah 65:18-19

13 But, according to his promise, we look for new heavens and a new earth, in which righteousness dwells.

2 Peter 3:13

5. You Will Become like Jesus

20 For our citizenship is in heaven, from where we also wait for a Savior, the Lord Jesus Christ, **21** who will change the body of our humiliation to be conformed to the body of his glory . . .

Philippians 3:20-21

4 When Christ, our life, is revealed, then you will also be revealed with him in glory.

Colossians 3:4

2 . . . but we know that when he is revealed, we will be like him; for we will see him just as he is.

1 John 3:2

3 Those who are wise will shine as the brightness of the expanse. Those who turn many to righteousness will shine as the stars forever and ever.

Daniel 12:3

43 Then the righteous will shine like the sun in the Kingdom of their Father.

Matthew 13:43

6. Death Is the Beginning of Heaven

50 Now I say this, brothers, that flesh and blood can't inherit God's Kingdom . . .

1 Corinthians 15:50

6 Therefore we are always confident and know that while we are at home in the body, we are absent from the Lord . . .

2 Corinthians 5:6

11 This saying is trustworthy: "For if we died with him, we will also live with him. **12** If we endure, we will also reign with him."

2 Timothy 2:11-12

8 For if we live, we live to the Lord. Or if we die, we die to the Lord. If therefore we live or die, we are the Lord's.

Romans 14:8

28 If you loved me, you would have rejoiced, because I said "I am going to my Father;" for the Father is greater than I.

John 14:28

13 I heard a voice from heaven saying, "Write, 'Blessed are the dead who die in the Lord from now on.'" "Yes," says the Spirit, "that they may rest from their labors; for their works follow with them."

Revelation 14:13

21 For to me to live is Christ, and to die is gain.

Philippians 1:21

23 But I am hard pressed between the two, having the desire to depart and be with Christ, which is far better.

Philippians 1:23

8 We are courageous, I say, and are willing rather to be absent from the body and to be at home with the Lord.

2 Corinthians 5:8

43 Jesus said to him, "Assuredly I tell you, today you will be with me in Paradise."

Luke 23:43

1 Don't let your heart be troubled. Believe in God. Believe also in me. **2** In my Father's house are many homes. If it weren't so, I would have told you. I am going to prepare a place for you. **3** If I go and prepare a place for you, I will come again, and will receive you to myself; that where I am, you may be there also.

John 14:1-3

7. Resurrection of Dead Believers

22 For as in Adam all die, so also in Christ all will be made alive. **23** But each in his own order: Christ the first fruits, then those who are Christ's, at his coming.

1 Corinthians 15:22-23

51 Behold, I tell you a mystery. We will not all sleep, but we will all be changed, **52** in a moment, in the twinkling of an eye, at the last trumpet. For the trumpet will sound and the dead will be raised incorruptible, and we will be changed.

1 Corinthians 15:51-52

16 For the Lord himself will descend from heaven with a shout, with the voice of the archangel and with God's trumpet. The dead in Christ will rise first, **17** then we who are alive, who are left, will be caught up together with them in the clouds, to meet the Lord in the air. So we will be with the Lord forever.

1 Thessalonians 4:16-17

4 When Christ, our life, is revealed, then you will also be revealed with him in glory.

Colossians 3:4

2 . . . but we know that when he is revealed, we will be like him; for we will see him just as he is.

1 John 3:2

42 So also is the resurrection of the dead. The body is sown perishable; it is raised imperishable. **43** It is sown in dishonor; it is raised in glory. It is sown in weakness; it is raised in power. **44** It is sown a natural body; it is raised a spiritual body. There is a natural body and there is also a spiritual body.

1 Corinthians 15:42-44

36 For they can't die any more, for they are like the angels, and are children of God, being children of the resurrection.

Luke 20:36

3 Those who are wise will shine as the brightness of the expanse. Those who turn many to righteousness will shine as the stars forever and ever.

Daniel 12:3

43 Then the righteous will shine like the sun in the Kingdom of their Father.

Matthew 13:43

8. The 1000-Year Kingdom before Heaven

28 so Christ also, having been offered once to bear the sins of many, will appear a second time, without sin, to those who are eagerly waiting for him for salvation.

Hebrews 9:28

44 In the days of those kings the God of heaven will set up a kingdom which will never be destroyed, nor will its sovereignty be left to another people . . .

Daniel 2:44

15 The kingdom of the world has become the Kingdom of our Lord, and of his Christ. He will reign forever and ever!

Revelation 11:15

9 . . . You are worthy to take the book and to open its seals: for you were killed, and bought us for God with your blood out of every tribe, language, people, and nation, **10** and made us kings and priests to our God, and we will reign on the earth.

Revelation 5:9-10

4 They lived and reigned with Christ for a thousand years.

Revelation 20:4

9. 1000 Years of Peace and Joy

28 so Christ also, having been offered once to bear the sins of many, will appear a second time, without sin, to those who are eagerly waiting for him for salvation.

Hebrews 9:28

44 In the days of those kings the God of heaven will set up a kingdom which will never be destroyed, nor will its sovereignty be left to another people . . .

Daniel 2:44

15 The kingdom of the world has become the Kingdom of our Lord, and of his Christ. He will reign forever and ever!

Revelation 11:15

9 . . . You are worthy to take the book and to open its seals: for you were killed, and bought us for God with your blood out of every tribe, language, people, and nation, **10** and made us kings and priests to our God, and we will reign on the earth.

Revelation 5:9-10

4 They lived and reigned with Christ for a thousand years.

Revelation 20:4

16 For the Lord himself will descend from heaven with a shout, with the voice of the archangel and with God's trumpet. The dead in Christ will rise first, **17** then we who are alive, who are left, will be caught up together with them in the clouds, to meet the Lord in the air. So we will be with the Lord forever.

1 Thessalonians 4:16-17

2 . . . we know that when he is revealed, we will be like him; for we will see him just as he is.

1 John 3:2

4 When Christ, our life, is revealed, then you will also be revealed with him in glory.

Colossians 3:4

42 So also is the resurrection of the dead. The body is sown perishable; it is raised imperishable. **43** It is sown in dishonor; it is raised in glory. It is sown in weakness; it is raised in power. **44** It is sown a natural body; it is raised a spiritual body. There is a natural body and there is also a spiritual body.

1 Corinthians 15:42-44

36 For they can't die any more, for they are like the angels, and are children of God, being children of the resurrection.

Luke 20:36

8 He has swallowed up death forever! The Lord GOD will wipe away tears from off all faces. He will take the reproach of his people away from off all the earth, for the LORD has spoken it. **9** It shall be said in that day, "Behold, this is our God! We have waited for him, and he will save us! This is the LORD! We have waited for him. We will be glad and rejoice in his salvation!"

Isaiah 25:8-9

2 It shall happen in the latter days, that the mountain of the LORD's house shall be established on the top of the mountains, and shall be raised above the hills; and all nations shall flow to it.

Isaiah 2:2

3 . . . For the law shall go out of Zion, and the LORD's word from Jerusalem. **4** He will judge between the nations, and will decide concerning many peoples. They shall beat their swords into ploughshares, and their spears into pruning hooks. Nation shall not lift up sword against nation, neither shall they learn war any more.

Isaiah 2:3-4

10 "Sing and rejoice, daughter of Zion! For behold, I come and I will dwell within you," says the LORD. **11** Many nations shall join themselves to the LORD in that day, and shall be my people; and I will dwell amongst you, and you shall know that the LORD of Armies has sent me to you. **12** The LORD will inherit Judah as his portion in the holy land, and will again choose Jerusalem.

Zechariah 2:10–12

9 For then I will purify the lips of the peoples, that they may all call on the LORD's name, to serve him shoulder to shoulder.

Zephaniah 3:9

18 Violence shall no more be heard in your land, nor desolation or destruction within your borders; but you will call your walls Salvation, and your gates Praise.

Isaiah 60:18

11 I tell you that many will come from the east and the west, and will sit down with Abraham, Isaac, and Jacob in the Kingdom of Heaven . . .

Matthew 8:11

6 In this mountain, the LORD of Armies will make all peoples a feast of choice meat, a feast of choice wines, of choice meat full of marrow, of well refined choice wines. . . **8** He has swallowed up death forever! . . . **9**

It shall be said in that day, "Behold, this is our God! We have waited for him, and he will save us! This is the LORD! We have waited for him. We will be glad and rejoice in his salvation!"

Isaiah 25:6,8-9

6 The wolf will live with the lamb, and the leopard will lie down with the young goat, the calf, the young lion, and the fattened calf together; and a little child will lead them. **7** The cow and the bear will graze. Their young ones will lie down together. The lion will eat straw like the ox.

Isaiah 11:6-7

8 The nursing child will play near a cobra's hole, and the weaned child will put his hand on the viper's den. **9** They will not hurt nor destroy in all my holy mountain; for the earth will be full of the knowledge of the LORD, as the waters cover the sea.

Isaiah 11:8-9

6 . . . Bring my sons from far away, and my daughters from the ends of the earth—**7** everyone who is called by my name, and whom I have created for my glory, whom I have formed, yes, whom I have made.

Isaiah 43:6-7

8 Behold, I will bring them from the north country, and gather them from the uttermost parts of the earth, along with the blind and the lame, the woman with child and her who travails with child together. They will return as a great company.

Jeremiah 31:8

5 Who is like the LORD, our God, who has his seat on high, **6** who stoops down to see in heaven and in the earth? **7** He raises up the poor out of the dust, and lifts up the needy from the ash heap, **8** that he may set him with princes, even with the princes of his people. **9** He settles the barren woman in her home as a joyful mother of children. Praise the LORD!

Psalm 113:5-9

5 . . . To him who loves us, and washed us from our sins by his blood— **6** and he made us to be a Kingdom, priests to his God and

Father—to him be the glory and the dominion forever and ever. Amen.

Revelation 1:5-6

26 You will have plenty to eat and be satisfied, and will praise the name of the LORD, your God, who has dealt wondrously with you; and my people will never again be disappointed.

Joel 2:26

10. Eternal Heaven: The New Jerusalem

1 I saw a new heaven and a new earth: for the first heaven and the first earth have passed away, and the sea is no more. **2** I saw the holy city, New Jerusalem, coming down out of heaven from God, prepared like a bride adorned for her husband.

Revelation 21:1-2

16 . . . because the former troubles are forgotten, and because they are hidden from my eyes. **17** For, behold, I create new heavens and a new earth; and the former things will not be remembered, nor come into mind.

Isaiah 65:16-17

18 But be glad and rejoice forever in that which I create; for, behold, I create Jerusalem to be a delight, and her people a joy. **19** I will rejoice in Jerusalem, and delight in my people; and the voice of weeping and the voice of crying will be heard in her no more.

Isaiah 65:18-19

1 I saw a new heaven and a new earth, for the first heaven and the first earth have passed away, and the sea is no more. **2** I saw the holy city, New Jerusalem, coming down out of heaven from God, prepared like a bride adorned for her husband.

Revelation 21:1–2

5 He who sits on the throne said, "Behold, I am making all things new." He said, "Write, for these words of God are faithful and true."

Revelation 21:5

3 I heard a loud voice out of heaven saying, "Behold, God's dwelling is with people, and he will dwell with them, and they will be his people, and God himself will be with them as their God. **4** He will wipe away every tear from their eyes. Death will be no more; neither will there be mourning, nor crying, nor pain, any more. The first things have passed away."

Revelation 21:3-4

10 He carried me away in the Spirit to a great and high mountain, and showed me the holy city, Jerusalem, coming down out of heaven from God, **11** having the glory of God. Her light was like a most precious stone, as if it were a jasper stone, clear as crystal . . .

Revelation 21:10-11

21 The twelve gates were twelve pearls. Each one of the gates was made of one pearl. The street of the city was pure gold, like transparent glass. **22** I saw no temple in it, for the Lord God, the Almighty, and the Lamb, are its temple.

Revelation 21:21-22

23 The city has no need for the sun or moon to shine, for the very glory of God illuminated it, and its lamp is the Lamb. **24** The nations will walk in its light. . .

Revelation 21:23-24

24 . . . The kings of the earth bring the glory and honor of the nations into it. **25** Its gates will in no way be shut by day (for there will be no night there), **26** and they shall bring the glory and the honor of the nations into it so that they may enter.

Revelation 21:24-26

1 He showed me a river of water of life, clear as crystal, proceeding out of the throne of God and of the Lamb, **2** in the middle of its street. On this side of the river and on that was the tree of life, bearing twelve kinds of fruits, yielding its fruit every month. The leaves of the tree were for the healing of the nations.

Revelation 22:1-2

3 There will be no curse any more. The throne of God and of the Lamb will be in it, and his servants will serve him. **4** They will see his face, and his name will be on their foreheads.

Revelation 22:3-4

5 There will be no night, and they need no lamp light or sun light; for the Lord God will illuminate them. They will reign forever and ever.

Revelation 22:5

11 I am coming quickly! Hold firmly that which you have, so that no one takes your crown. **12** He who overcomes, I will make him a pillar in the temple of my God, and he will go out from there no more. I will write on him the name of my God and the name of the city of my God, the new Jerusalem, which comes down out of heaven from my God, and my own new name.

Revelation 3:11-12

24 Father, I desire that they also whom you have given me be with me where I am, that they may see my glory, which you have given me, for you loved me before the foundation of the world.

John 17:24

20 . . . but rejoice that your names are written in heaven.

Luke 10:20

3 Blessed be the God and Father of our Lord Jesus Christ, who according to his great mercy caused us to be born again to a living hope through the resurrection of Jesus Christ from the dead, **4** to an incorruptible and undefiled inheritance that doesn't fade away, reserved in Heaven for you . . .

1 Peter 1:3-4

13 But now faith, hope, and love remain—these three. The greatest of these is love. **1** Follow after love . . .

1 Corinthians 13:13-14:1

4. True, Eternal Hope

1. You Are in Good Hands

3 But the Lord is faithful, who will establish you and guard you from the evil one.

2 Thessalonians 3:3

4 I tell you, my friends, don't be afraid of those who kill the body, and after that have no more that they can do.

Luke 12:4

28 Don't be afraid of those who kill the body, but are not able to kill the soul. Rather, fear him who is able to destroy both soul and body in Gehenna.

Matthew 10:28

11 Jesus answered, "You would have no power at all against me, unless it were given to you from above."

John 19:11

5 I will in no way leave you, neither will I in any way forsake you.

Hebrews 13:5

20 Behold, I am with you always, even to the end of the age.

Matthew 28:20

4 Even though I walk through the valley of the shadow of death, I will fear no evil, for you are with me.

Psalm 23:4

10 Don't you be afraid, for I am with you. Don't be dismayed, for I am your God. I will strengthen you. Yes, I will help you. Yes, I will uphold you with the right hand of my righteousness.

Isaiah 41:10

18 And the Lord will deliver me from every evil work, and will preserve me for his heavenly Kingdom. To him be the glory forever and ever. Amen.

2 Timothy 4:18

27 My sheep hear my voice, and I know them, and they follow me. **28** I give eternal life to them. They will never perish, and no one will snatch them out of my hand. **29** My Father who has given them to me is greater than all. No one is able to snatch them out of my Father's hand.

John 10:27-29

38 For I am persuaded that neither death, nor life, nor angels, nor principalities, nor things present, nor things to come, nor powers, **39** nor height, nor depth, nor any other created thing will be able to separate us from God's love which is in Christ Jesus our Lord.

Romans 8:38-39

7 The LORD will keep you from all evil. He will keep your soul. **8** The LORD will keep your going out and your coming in, from this time forward, and forever more.

Psalm 121:7-8

19 Many are the afflictions of the righteous, but the LORD delivers him out of them all.

Psalm 34:19

37 No, in all these things, we are more than conquerors through him who loved us.

Romans 8:37

57 But thanks be to God, who gives us the victory through our Lord Jesus Christ.

1 Corinthians 15:57

2. Your True Hope Is Heaven

7 For we brought nothing into the world, and we certainly can't carry anything out.

1 Timothy 6:7

7 But the heavens that exist now and the earth, by the same word have been stored up for fire . . .

2 Peter 3:7

26 For what will it profit a man if he gains the whole world and forfeits his life?

Matthew 16:26

24 . . . but hope that is seen is not hope. For who hopes for that which he sees?

Romans 8:24

13 But, according to his promise, we look for new heavens and a new earth, in which righteousness dwells.

2 Peter 3:13

18 while we don't look at the things which are seen, but at the things which are not seen. For the things which are seen are temporal, but the things which are not seen are eternal.

2 Corinthians 4:18

20 . . . but rejoice that your names are written in heaven.

Luke 10:20

20 For our citizenship is in heaven, from where we also wait for a Savior, the Lord Jesus Christ . . .

Philippians 3:20

18 And the Lord will deliver me from every evil work, and will preserve me for his heavenly Kingdom. To him be the glory forever and ever. Amen.

2 Timothy 4:18

41 Jesus answered her, "Martha, Martha, you are anxious and troubled about many things, **42** but one thing is needed. Mary has chosen the good part, which will not be taken away from her."

Luke 10:41-42

3. Your True Home Is Heaven

20 Jesus said to him, "The foxes have holes and the birds of the sky have nests, but the Son of Man has nowhere to lay his head."

Matthew 8:20

36 Jesus answered, "My Kingdom is not of this world. . . But now my Kingdom is not from here."

John 18:36

37 . . . They went around in sheep skins and in goat skins; being destitute, afflicted, ill-treated— **38** of whom the world was not worthy—wandering in deserts, mountains, caves, and the holes of the earth.

Hebrews 11:37-38

1 For we know that if the earthly house of our tent is dissolved, we have a building from God, a house not made with hands, eternal, in the heavens.

2 Corinthians 5:1

20 For our citizenship is in heaven, from where we also wait for a Savior, the Lord Jesus Christ, **21** who will change the body of our humiliation to be conformed to the body of his glory . . .

Philippians 3:20-21

20 . . . but rejoice that your names are written in heaven.

Luke 10:20

7 But the heavens that exist now and the earth, by the same word have been stored up for fire . . .

2 Peter 3:7

13 But, according to his promise, we look for new heavens and a new earth, in which righteousness dwells.

2 Peter 3:13

24 . . . but hope that is seen is not hope. For who hopes for that which he sees?

Romans 8:24

18 while we don't look at the things which are seen, but at the things which are not seen. For the things which are seen are temporal, but the things which are not seen are eternal.

2 Corinthians 4:18

17 If you call on him as Father, who without respect of persons judges according to each man's work, pass the time of your living as foreigners here in reverent fear . . .

1 Peter 1:17

1 If then you were raised together with Christ, seek the things that are above, where Christ is, seated on the right hand of God. **2** Set your mind on the things that are above, not on the things that are on the earth.

Colossians 3:1–2

13 But now faith, hope, and love remain—these three. The greatest of these is love. **1** Follow after love . . .

1 Corinthians 13:13-14:1

4. Dying Is Being with God

50 Now I say this, brothers, that flesh and blood can't inherit God's Kingdom . . .

1 Corinthians 15:50

6 Therefore we are always confident and know that while we are at home in the body, we are absent from the Lord . . .

2 Corinthians 5:6

8 We are courageous, I say, and are willing rather to be absent from the body and to be at home with the Lord.

2 Corinthians 5:8

23 But I am hard pressed between the two, having the desire to depart and be with Christ, which is far better.

Philippians 1:23

28 If you loved me, you would have rejoiced, because I said "I am going to my Father;" for the Father is greater than I.

John 14:28

43 Jesus said to him, "Assuredly I tell you, today you will be with me in Paradise."

Luke 23:43

1 Don't let your heart be troubled. Believe in God. Believe also in me. **2** In my Father's house are many homes. If it weren't so, I would have told you. I am going to prepare a place for you. **3** If I go and prepare a place for you, I will come again, and will receive you to myself; that where I am, you may be there also.

John 14:1-3

5. Death Is Gain

21 For to me to live is Christ, and to die is gain.

Philippians 1:21

23 But I am hard pressed between the two, having the desire to depart and be with Christ, which is far better.

Philippians 1:23

13 I heard a voice from heaven saying, "Write, 'Blessed are the dead who die in the Lord from now on.'" "Yes," says the Spirit, "that they may rest from their labors; for their works follow with them."

Revelation 14:13

43 Jesus said to him, "Assuredly I tell you, today you will be with me in Paradise."

Luke 23:43

28 If you loved me, you would have rejoiced, because I said "I am going to my Father;" for the Father is greater than I.

John 14:28

6. Meeting Your Loved One Again

23 But now he is dead. Why should I fast? Can I bring him back again? I will go to him, but he will not return to me.

2 Samuel 12:23

2 Therefore I praised the dead who have been long dead more than the living who are yet alive. **3** Yes, better than them both is him who has not yet been, who has not seen the evil work that is done under the sun.

Ecclesiastes 4:2–3

16 A little while, and you will not see me. Again a little while, and you will see me.

John 16:16

17 Some of his disciples therefore said to one another, "What is this that he says to us, 'A little while, and you won't see me, and again a little while, and you will see me;' and, 'Because I go to the Father'?"

John 16:17

20 Most certainly I tell you that you will weep and lament, but the world will rejoice. You will be sorrowful, but your sorrow will be turned into joy.

John 16:20

22 Therefore you now have sorrow, but I will see you again, and your heart will rejoice, and no one will take your joy away from you.

John 16:22

4 By faith Abel offered to God a more excellent sacrifice than Cain, through which he had testimony given to him that he was righteous, God testifying with respect to his gifts; and through it he, being dead, still speaks.

Hebrews 11:4

7. God's Eternal Restoration

4 Blessed are those who mourn, for they shall be comforted.

Matthew 5:4

21 Blessed are you who hunger now, for you will be filled. Blessed are you who weep now, for you will laugh.

Luke 6:21

16 The LORD says: "Refrain your voice from weeping, and your eyes from tears, for your work will be rewarded," says the LORD.

Jeremiah 31:16

14 But you do see trouble and grief. You consider it to take it into your hand. You help the victim and the fatherless.

Psalm 10:14

24 For he has not despised nor abhorred the affliction of the afflicted, neither has he hidden his face from him; but when he cried to him, he heard.

Psalm 22:24

25 I will restore to you the years that the swarming locust has eaten, the great locust, the grasshopper, and the caterpillar, my great army, which I sent amongst you.

Joel 2:25

11 In that day I will raise up the tent of David who is fallen and close up its breaches, and I will raise up its ruins, and I will build it as in the days of old . . .

Amos 9:11

10 Then the LORD's ransomed ones will return, and come with singing to Zion; and everlasting joy will be on their heads. They will obtain gladness and joy, and sorrow and sighing will flee away.

Isaiah 35:10

5 Those who sow in tears will reap in joy. **6** He who goes out weeping, carrying seed for sowing, will certainly come again with joy, carrying his sheaves.

Psalm 126:5-6

8 Behold, I will bring them from the north country, and gather them from the uttermost parts of the earth, along with the blind and the lame, the woman with child and her who travails with child together. They will return as a great company.

Jeremiah 31:8

5 Who is like the LORD, our God, who has his seat on high, **6** who stoops down to see in heaven and in the earth? **7** He raises up the poor out of the dust, and lifts up the needy from the ash heap, **8** that he may set him with princes, even with the princes of his people. **9** He settles the barren woman in her home as a joyful mother of children. Praise the LORD!

Psalm 113:5-9

6 "In that day," says the LORD, "I will assemble that which is lame, and I will gather that which is driven away, and that which I have afflicted; **7** and I will make that which was lame a remnant, and that which was cast far off a strong nation: and the LORD will reign over them on Mount Zion from then on, even forever."

Micah 4:6–7

1 When the LORD brought back those who returned to Zion, we were like those who dream. **2** Then our mouth was filled with laughter, and our tongue with singing. Then they said amongst the nations, "The LORD has done great things for them." **3** The LORD has done great things for us, and we are glad.

Psalm 126:1-3

20 . . . Surely he has done great things. **21** Land, don't be afraid. Be glad and rejoice, for the LORD has done great things. **22** Don't be afraid, you animals of the field; for the pastures of the wilderness spring up, for the tree bears its fruit. The fig tree and the vine yield their strength.

Joel 2:20-22

12 They will come and sing in the height of Zion, and will flow to the goodness of the LORD, to the grain, to the new wine, to the oil, and to the young of the flock and of the herd. Their soul will be as a watered garden. They will not sorrow any more at all. **13** Then the virgin will rejoice in the dance, the young men and the old together; for I will turn their mourning into joy, and will comfort them, and make them rejoice from their sorrow.

Jeremiah 31:12-13

16 . . . because the former troubles are forgotten, and because they are hidden from my eyes. **17** For, behold, I create new heavens and a new earth; and the former things will not be remembered, nor come into mind. **18** But be glad and rejoice forever in that which I create; for, behold,

I create Jerusalem to be a delight, and her people a joy. **19** I will rejoice in Jerusalem, and delight in my people; and the voice of weeping and the voice of crying will be heard in her no more.

Isaiah 65:16-19

16 They will never be hungry or thirsty any more. The sun won't beat on them, nor any heat; **17** for the Lamb who is in the middle of the throne shepherds them and leads them to springs of life-giving waters. And God will wipe away every tear from their eyes.

Revelation 7:16-17

3 I heard a loud voice out of heaven saying, "Behold, God's dwelling is with people, and he will dwell with them, and they will be his people, and God himself will be with them as their God. **4** He will wipe away every tear from their eyes. Death will be no more; neither will there be mourning, nor crying, nor pain, any more. The first things have passed away."

Revelation 21:3-4

8 He has swallowed up death forever! The Lord GOD will wipe away tears from off all faces. He will take the reproach of his people away from off all the earth, for the LORD has spoken it. **9** It shall be said in that day, "Behold, this is our God! We have waited for him, and he will save us! This is the LORD! We have waited for him. We will be glad and rejoice in his salvation!"

Isaiah 25:8-9

20 Most certainly I tell you that you will weep and lament, but the world will rejoice. You will be sorrowful, but your sorrow will be turned into joy.

John 16:20

22 Therefore you now have sorrow, but I will see you again, and your heart will rejoice, and no one will take your joy away from you.

John 16:22

3 There will be no curse any more. The throne of God and of the Lamb will be in it, and his servants will serve him. **4** They will see his face, and his name will be on their foreheads. **5** There will be no night, and they need no lamp light or sun light; for the Lord God will illuminate them. They will reign forever and ever.

Revelation 22:3-5

16 They will never be hungry or thirsty any more. The sun won't beat on them, nor any heat; **17** for the Lamb who is in the middle of the throne shepherds them and leads them to springs of life-giving waters. And God will wipe away every tear from their eyes.

Revelation 7:16-17

1 The Lord GOD's Spirit is on me, because the LORD has anointed me to preach good news to the humble. He has sent me to bind up the broken hearted, to proclaim liberty to the captives and release to those who are bound, **2** to proclaim the year of the LORD's favour and the day of vengeance of our God, to comfort all who mourn, **3** to provide for those who mourn in Zion, to give to them a garland for ashes, the oil of joy for mourning, the garment of praise for the spirit of heaviness, that they may be called trees of righteousness, the planting of the LORD, that he may be glorified.

Isaiah 61:1-3

8. You Will See Jesus Forever

1 Don't let your heart be troubled. Believe in God. Believe also in me. **2** In my Father's house are many homes. If it weren't so, I would have told you. I am going to prepare a place for you. **3** If I go and prepare a place for you, I will come again, and will receive you to myself; that where I am, you may be there also.

John 14:1-3

20 For our citizenship is in heaven, from where we also wait for a Savior, the Lord Jesus Christ, **21** who will change the body of our humiliation to be conformed to the body of his glory, according to the working by which he is able even to subject all things to himself.

Philippians 3:20-21

20 . . . but rejoice that your names are written in heaven.

Luke 10:20

2 . . . we know that when he is revealed, we will be like him; for we will see him just as he is.

1 John 3:2

4 When Christ, our life, is revealed, then you will also be revealed with him in glory.

Colossians 3:4

3 There will be no curse any more. The throne of God and of the Lamb will be in it, and his servants will serve him. **4** They will see his face, and his name will be on their foreheads.

Revelation 22:3-4

9 It shall be said in that day, "Behold, this is our God! We have waited for him, and he will save us! This is the LORD! We have waited for him. We will be glad and rejoice in his salvation!"

Isaiah 25:9

17 . . . So we will be with the Lord forever.

1 Thessalonians 4:17

43 Jesus said to him, "Assuredly I tell you, today you will be with me in Paradise."

Luke 23:43

9. Heaven Is Eternal Paradise

16 . . . because the former troubles are forgotten, and because they are hidden from my eyes. **17** For, behold, I create new heavens and a new earth; and the former things will not be remembered, nor come into mind.

Isaiah 65:16-17

4 He will wipe away every tear from their eyes. Death will be no more; neither will there be mourning, nor crying, nor pain, any more. The first things have passed away.

Revelation 21:4

5 He who sits on the throne said, "Behold, I am making all things new." He said,

"Write, for these words of God are faithful and true."

Revelation 21:5

4 When Christ, our life, is revealed, then you will also be revealed with him in glory.

Colossians 3:4

2 . . . we know that when he is revealed, we will be like him; for we will see him just as he is.

1 John 3:2

42 So also is the resurrection of the dead. The body is sown perishable; it is raised imperishable. **43** It is sown in dishonor; it is raised in glory. It is sown in weakness; it is raised in power. **44** It is sown a natural body; it is raised a spiritual body. There is a natural body and there is also a spiritual body.

1 Corinthians 15:42-44

36 For they can't die any more, for they are like the angels, and are children of God, being children of the resurrection.

Luke 20:36

9 It shall be said in that day, "Behold, this is our God! We have waited for him, and he will save us! This is the LORD! We have waited for him. We will be glad and rejoice in his salvation!"

Isaiah 25:9

17 . . . So we will be with the Lord forever.

1 Thessalonians 4:17

43 Jesus said to him, "Assuredly I tell you, today you will be with me in Paradise."

Luke 23:43

1 I saw a new heaven and a new earth, for the first heaven and the first earth have passed away, and the sea is no more. **2** I saw the holy city, New Jerusalem, coming down out of heaven from God, prepared like a bride adorned for her husband.

Revelation 21:1–2

18 But be glad and rejoice forever in that which I create; for, behold, I create Jerusalem to be a delight, and her people a joy. **19** I will rejoice in Jerusalem, and delight in my people; and the voice of weeping and the voice of crying will be heard in her no more.

Isaiah 65:18-19

11 I am coming quickly! Hold firmly that which you have, so that no one takes your crown. **12** He who overcomes, I will make him a pillar in the temple of my God, and he will go out from there no more. I will write on him the name of my God and the name of the city of my God, the new Jerusalem, which comes down out of heaven from my God, and my own new name.

Revelation 3:11-12

21 He who overcomes, I will give to him to sit down with me on my throne, as I also overcame, and sat down with my Father on his throne.

Revelation 3:21

7 He who overcomes, I will give him these things. I will be his God, and he will be my son.

Revelation 21:7

23 The city has no need for the sun or moon to shine, for the very glory of God illuminated it, and its lamp is the Lamb. **24** The nations will walk in its light. . .

Revelation 21:23-24

3 There will be no curse any more. The throne of God and of the Lamb will be in it, and his servants will serve him. **4** They will see his face, and his name will be on their foreheads.

Revelation 22:3-4

5 There will be no night, and they need no lamp light or sun light; for the Lord God will illuminate them. They will reign forever and ever.

Revelation 22:5

3 Those who are wise will shine as the brightness of the expanse. Those who turn many to righteousness will shine as the stars forever and ever.

Daniel 12:3

43 Then the righteous will shine like the sun in the Kingdom of their Father.

Matthew 13:43

10. Your Eternal Reward

16 The LORD says: "Refrain your voice from weeping, and your eyes from tears, for your work will be rewarded," says the LORD.

Jeremiah 31:16

18 And the Lord will deliver me from every evil work, and will preserve me for his heavenly Kingdom. To him be the glory forever and ever. Amen.

2 Timothy 4:18

17 For our light affliction, which is for the moment, works for us more and more exceedingly an eternal weight of glory . . .

2 Corinthians 4:17

18 For I consider that the sufferings of this present time are not worthy to be compared with the glory which will be revealed toward us.

Romans 8:18

21 His lord said to him, "Well done, good and faithful servant. You have been faithful over a few things, I will set you over many things. Enter into the joy of your lord."

Matthew 25:21

4 For whatever is born of God overcomes the world. This is the victory that has overcome the world: your faith. **5** Who is he who overcomes the world, but he who believes that Jesus is the Son of God?

1 John 5:4-5

7 To him who overcomes I will give to eat from the tree of life, which is in the Paradise of my God.

Revelation 2:7

11 He who overcomes won't be harmed by the second death.

Revelation 2:11

17 To him who overcomes, to him I will give of the hidden manna, and I will give him a white stone, and on the stone a new name written, which no one knows but he who receives it.

Revelation 2:17

25 Nevertheless, hold that which you have firmly until I come. **26** He who overcomes, and he who keeps my works to the end, to him I will give authority over the nations. **27** He will rule them with a rod of iron, shattering them like clay pots; as I also have received of my Father: **28** and I will give him the morning star.

Revelation 2:25-28

5 He who overcomes will be arrayed in white garments, and I will in no way blot his name out of the book of life, and I will confess his name before my Father, and before his angels.

Revelation 3:5

11 I am coming quickly! Hold firmly that which you have, so that no one takes your crown. **12** He who overcomes, I will make him a pillar in the temple of my God, and he will go out from there no more. I will write on him the name of my God and the name of the city of my God, the new Jerusalem, which comes down out of heaven from my God, and my own new name.

Revelation 3:11-12

21 He who overcomes, I will give to him to sit down with me on my throne, as I also overcame, and sat down with my Father on his throne.

Revelation 3:21

7 He who overcomes, I will give him these things. I will be his God, and he will be my son.

Revelation 21:7

4 When Christ, our life, is revealed, then you will also be revealed with him in glory.

Colossians 3:4

2 . . . we know that when he is revealed, we will be like him; for we will see him just as he is.

1 John 3:2

16 . . . because the former troubles are forgotten, and because they are hidden from my eyes. **17** For, behold, I create new heavens and a new earth; and the former things will not be remembered, nor come into mind.

Isaiah 65:16-17

4 He will wipe away every tear from their eyes. Death will be no more; neither will there be mourning, nor crying, nor pain, any more. The first things have passed away.

Revelation 21:4

3 There will be no curse any more. The throne of God and of the Lamb will be in it, and his servants will serve him. **4** They will see his face, and his name will be on their foreheads. **5** There will be no night, and they need no lamp light or sun light; for the Lord God will illuminate them. They will reign forever and ever.

Revelation 22:3-5

3 Those who are wise will shine as the brightness of the expanse. Those who turn many to righteousness will shine as the stars forever and ever.

Daniel 12:3

43 Then the righteous will shine like the sun in the Kingdom of their Father.

Matthew 13:43

37 No, in all these things, we are more than conquerors through him who loved us.

Romans 8:37

57 But thanks be to God, who gives us the victory through our Lord Jesus Christ.

1 Corinthians 15:57

11. God's Eternal Promise of Hope

18 And the Lord will deliver me from every evil work, and will preserve me for his heavenly Kingdom. To him be the glory forever and ever. Amen.

2 Timothy 4:18

20 . . . but rejoice that your names are written in heaven.

Luke 10:20

20 For our citizenship is in heaven, from where we also wait for a Savior, the Lord Jesus Christ, **21** who will change the body of our humiliation to be conformed to the body of his glory . . .

Philippians 3:20-21

3 Blessed be the God and Father of our Lord Jesus Christ, who according to his great mercy caused us to be born again to a living hope through the resurrection of Jesus Christ from the dead, **4** to an incorruptible and undefiled inheritance that doesn't fade away, reserved in Heaven for you . . .

1 Peter 1:3-4

1 Don't let your heart be troubled. Believe in God. Believe also in me. **2** In my Father's house are many homes. If it weren't so, I would have told you. I am going to prepare a place for you. **3** If I go and prepare a place for you, I will come again, and will receive you to myself; that where I am, you may be there also.

John 14:1-3

12. What Is Heaven Like?

1 I saw a new heaven and a new earth, for the first heaven and the first earth have passed away, and the sea is no more. **2** I saw the holy city, New Jerusalem, coming down out of heaven from God, prepared like a bride adorned for her husband.

Revelation 21:1–2

16 . . . because the former troubles are forgotten, and because they are hidden from my eyes. **17** For, behold, I create new heavens and a new earth; and the former things will not be remembered, nor come into mind.

Isaiah 65:16-17

18 But be glad and rejoice forever in that which I create; for, behold, I create Jerusalem to be a delight, and her people a joy. **19** I will rejoice in Jerusalem, and delight in my people; and the voice of weeping and the voice of crying will be heard in her no more.

Isaiah 65:18-19

5 He who sits on the throne said, "Behold, I am making all things new." He said, "Write, for these words of God are faithful and true."

Revelation 21:5

3 I heard a loud voice out of heaven saying, "Behold, God's dwelling is with people, and he will dwell with them, and they will be his people, and God himself will be with them as their God. **4** He will wipe away every tear from their eyes. Death will be no more; neither will there be mourning, nor crying, nor pain, any more. The first things have passed away."

Revelation 21:3-4

10 He carried me away in the Spirit to a great and high mountain, and showed me the holy city, Jerusalem, coming down out of heaven from God, **11** having the glory of God. Her light was like a most precious stone, as if it were a jasper stone, clear as crystal . . .

Revelation 21:10-11

21 The twelve gates were twelve pearls. Each one of the gates was made of one pearl. The street of the city was pure gold, like transparent glass. **22** I saw no temple in it, for the Lord God, the Almighty, and the Lamb, are its temple.

Revelation 21:21-22

23 The city has no need for the sun or moon to shine, for the very glory of God illuminated it, and its lamp is the Lamb. **24** The nations will walk in its light. . .

Revelation 21:23-24

24 . . . The kings of the earth bring the glory and honor of the nations into it. **25** Its gates will in no way be shut by day (for there will be no night there), **26** and they shall bring the glory and the honor of the nations into it so that they may enter.

Revelation 21:24-26

1 He showed me a river of water of life, clear as crystal, proceeding out of the throne of God and of the Lamb, **2** in the middle of its street. On this side of the river and on that was the tree of life, bearing twelve kinds of fruits, yielding its fruit every month. The leaves of the tree were for the healing of the nations.

Revelation 22:1-2

3 There will be no curse any more. The throne of God and of the Lamb will be in it, and his servants will serve him. **4** They will see his face, and his name will be on their foreheads.

Revelation 22:3-4

5 There will be no night, and they need no lamp light or sun light; for the Lord God will illuminate them. They will reign forever and ever.

Revelation 22:5

11 I am coming quickly! Hold firmly that which you have, so that no one takes your crown. **12** He who overcomes, I will make him a pillar in the temple of my God, and he will go out from there no more. I will write on him the name of my God and the name of the city of my God, the new Jerusalem, which comes down out of heaven from my God, and my own new name.

Revelation 3:11-12

7 He who overcomes, I will give him these things. I will be his God, and he will be my son.

Revelation 21:7

24 Father, I desire that they also whom you have given me be with me where I am, that they may see my glory, which you have given me, for you loved me before the foundation of the world.

John 17:24

20 . . . but rejoice that your names are written in heaven.

Luke 10:20

3 Blessed be the God and Father of our Lord Jesus Christ, who according to his great mercy caused us to be born again to a living hope through the resurrection of Jesus Christ from the dead, **4** to an incorruptible and undefiled inheritance that doesn't fade away, reserved in Heaven for you . . .

1 Peter 1:3-4

20 For our citizenship is in heaven, from where we also wait for a Savior, the Lord Jesus Christ, **21** who will change the body of our humiliation to be conformed to the body of his glory . . .

Philippians 3:20-21

11 "He who acts unjustly, let him act unjustly still. He who is filthy, let him be filthy still. He who is righteous, let him do righteousness still. He who is holy, let him be holy still." **12** "Behold, I am coming soon! My reward is with me, to repay to each man according to his work. **13** I am the Alpha and the Omega, the First and the Last, the Beginning and the End."

Revelation 22:11–13

14 Blessed are those who do his commandments, that they may have the right to the tree of life, and may enter in by the gates into the city. **15** Outside are the dogs, the sorcerers, the sexually immoral, the murderers, the idolaters, and everyone who loves and practices falsehood. **16** I, Jesus, have sent my angel to testify these things to you for the assemblies. I am the root and the offspring of David, the Bright and Morning Star.

Revelation 22:14–16

20 He who testifies these things says, "Yes, I am coming soon." Amen! Yes, come, Lord Jesus! **21** The grace of the Lord Jesus Christ be with all the saints. Amen.

Revelation 22:20–21

13 But now faith, hope, and love remain—these three. The greatest of these is love. **1** Follow after love . . .

1 Corinthians 13:13-14:1

13. Heaven Is Where God Lives

1 The LORD says: "Heaven is my throne, and the earth is my footstool."

Isaiah 66:1

15 For the high and lofty One who inhabits eternity, whose name is Holy, says: "I dwell in the high and holy place . . ."

Isaiah 57:15

5 This is the message which we have heard from him and announce to you, that God is light, and in him is no darkness at all.

1 John 1:5

17 for God's Kingdom is not eating and drinking, but righteousness, peace, and joy in the Holy Spirit.

Romans 14:17

14 But Jesus said, "Allow the little children, and don't forbid them to come to me; for the Kingdom of Heaven belongs to ones like these."

Matthew 19:14

15 Most certainly I tell you, whoever will not receive God's Kingdom like a little child, he will in no way enter into it.

Mark 10:15

14. Eternal Heaven: The New Jerusalem

1 I saw a new heaven and a new earth: for the first heaven and the first earth have passed away, and the sea is no more. **2** I saw the holy city, New Jerusalem, coming down out of heaven from God, prepared like a bride adorned for her husband.

Revelation 21:1-2

16 . . . because the former troubles are forgotten, and because they are hidden from my eyes. **17** For, behold, I create new heavens and a new earth; and the former things will not be remembered, nor come into mind.

Isaiah 65:16-17

18 But be glad and rejoice forever in that which I create; for, behold, I create Jerusalem to be a delight, and her people a joy. **19** I will rejoice in Jerusalem, and delight in my people; and the voice of weeping and the voice of crying will be heard in her no more.

Isaiah 65:18-19

1 I saw a new heaven and a new earth, for the first heaven and the first earth have passed away, and the sea is no more. **2** I saw the holy city, New Jerusalem, coming down out of heaven from God, prepared like a bride adorned for her husband.

Revelation 21:1–2

5 He who sits on the throne said, "Behold, I am making all things new." He said, "Write, for these words of God are faithful and true."

Revelation 21:5

3 I heard a loud voice out of heaven saying, "Behold, God's dwelling is with people, and he will dwell with them, and they will be his people, and God himself will be with them as their God. **4** He will wipe away every tear from their eyes. Death will be no more; neither will there be mourning, nor crying, nor pain, any more. The first things have passed away."

Revelation 21:3-4

10 He carried me away in the Spirit to a great and high mountain, and showed me the holy city, Jerusalem, coming down out of heaven from God, **11** having the glory of God. Her light was like a most precious stone, as if it were a jasper stone, clear as crystal . . .

Revelation 21:10-11

21 The twelve gates were twelve pearls. Each one of the gates was made of one pearl. The street of the city was pure gold, like transparent glass. **22** I saw no temple in it, for the Lord God, the Almighty, and the Lamb, are its temple.

Revelation 21:21-22

23 The city has no need for the sun or moon to shine, for the very glory of God illuminated it, and its lamp is the Lamb. **24** The nations will walk in its light. . .

Revelation 21:23-24

24 . . . The kings of the earth bring the glory and honor of the nations into it. **25** Its gates will in no way be shut by day (for there will be no night there), **26** and they shall bring the glory and the honor of the nations into it so that they may enter.

Revelation 21:24-26

1 He showed me a river of water of life, clear as crystal, proceeding out of the throne of God and of the Lamb, **2** in the middle of its street. On this side of the river and on that was the tree of life, bearing twelve kinds of fruits, yielding its fruit every month. The leaves of the tree were for the healing of the nations.

Revelation 22:1-2

3 There will be no curse any more. The throne of God and of the Lamb will be in it, and his servants will serve him. **4** They will see his face, and his name will be on their foreheads.

Revelation 22:3-4

5 There will be no night, and they need no lamp light or sun light; for the Lord God will illuminate them. They will reign forever and ever.

Revelation 22:5

11 I am coming quickly! Hold firmly that which you have, so that no one takes your crown. **12** He who overcomes, I will make him a pillar in the temple of my God, and he will go out from there no more. I will write on him the name of my God and the name of the city of my God, the new Jerusalem, which comes down out of heaven from my God, and my own new name.

Revelation 3:11-12

24 Father, I desire that they also whom you have given me be with me where I am, that they may see my glory, which you have given me, for you loved me before the foundation of the world.

John 17:24

20 . . . but rejoice that your names are written in heaven.

Luke 10:20

3 Blessed be the God and Father of our Lord Jesus Christ, who according to his great mercy caused us to be born again to a living hope through the resurrection of Jesus Christ from the dead, **4** to an incorruptible and undefiled inheritance that doesn't fade away, reserved in Heaven for you . . .

1 Peter 1:3-4

13 But now faith, hope, and love remain—these three. The greatest of these is love. **1** Follow after love . . .

1 Corinthians 13:13-14:1

15. The Promised Eternal Hope

18 And the Lord will deliver me from every evil work, and will preserve me for his heavenly Kingdom. To him be the glory forever and ever. Amen.

2 Timothy 4:18

20 . . . but rejoice that your names are written in heaven.

Luke 10:20

20 For our citizenship is in heaven, from where we also wait for a Savior, the Lord Jesus Christ, **21** who will change the body of our humiliation to be conformed to the body of his glory . . .

Philippians 3:20-21

3 Blessed be the God and Father of our Lord Jesus Christ, who according to his great mercy caused us to be born again to a living hope through the resurrection of Jesus Christ from the dead, **4** to an incorruptible and undefiled inheritance that doesn't fade away, reserved in Heaven for you . . .

1 Peter 1:3-4

16 . . . because the former troubles are forgotten, and because they are hidden from my eyes. **17** For, behold, I create new heavens and a new earth; and the former things will not be remembered, nor come into mind.

Isaiah 65:16-17

4 He will wipe away every tear from their eyes. Death will be no more; neither will there be mourning, nor crying, nor pain, any more. The first things have passed away.

Revelation 21:4

3 There will be no curse any more. The throne of God and of the Lamb will be in it, and his servants will serve him. **4** They will see his face, and his name will be on their foreheads.

Revelation 22:3-4

5 There will be no night, and they need no lamp light or sun light; for the Lord God will illuminate them. They will reign forever and ever.

Revelation 22:5

3 Those who are wise will shine as the brightness of the expanse. Those who turn many to righteousness will shine as the stars forever and ever.

Daniel 12:3

43 Then the righteous will shine like the sun in the Kingdom of their Father.

Matthew 13:43

1 Don't let your heart be troubled. Believe in God. Believe also in me. **2** In my Father's house are many homes. If it weren't so, I would have told you. I am going to prepare a place for you. **3** If I go and prepare a place for you, I will come again, and will receive you to myself; that where I am, you may be there also.

John 14:1-3

5. It Doesn't Matter How You Die

1. We All Die

15 Precious in the LORD's sight is the death of his saints.

Psalm 116:15

14 He will redeem their soul from oppression and violence. Their blood will be precious in his sight.

Psalm 72:14

20 All go to one place. All are from the dust, and all turn to dust again.

Ecclesiastes 3:20

7 and the dust returns to the earth as it was, and the spirit returns to God who gave it.

Ecclesiastes 12:7

27 Inasmuch as it is appointed for men to die once, and after this, judgment . . .

Hebrews 9:27

1 For everything there is a season, and a time for every purpose under heaven: **2** a time to be born, and a time to die; a time to plant, and a time to pluck up that which is planted . . .

Ecclesiastes 3:1–2

1 A good name is better than fine perfume; and the day of death better than the day of one's birth. **2** It is better to go to the house of mourning than to go to the house of feasting; for that is the end of all men, and the living should take this to heart.

Ecclesiastes 7:1–2

2. God's People Die in Different Ways

14 Now Elisha became sick with the illness of which he died . . .

2 Kings 13:14

37 They were stoned. They were sawn apart. They were tempted. They were slain with the sword. They went around in sheep skins and in goat skins; being destitute, afflicted, ill-treated— **38** of whom the world was not worthy—wandering in deserts, mountains, caves, and the holes of the earth.

Hebrews 11:37–38

27 Immediately the king sent out a soldier of his guard and commanded to bring John's head; and he went and beheaded him in the prison, **28** and brought his head on a platter, and gave it to the young lady; and the young lady gave it to her mother. **29** When his disciples heard this, they came and took up his corpse and laid it in a tomb.

Mark 6:27–29

3. Jesus Died a Horrible Death

33 Behold, we are going up to Jerusalem. The Son of Man will be delivered to the chief priests and the scribes. They will condemn him to death, and will deliver him to the Gentiles. **34** They will mock him, spit on him, scourge him, and kill him. On the third day he will rise again.

Mark 10:33-34

66 They answered, "He is worthy of death!" **67** Then they spat in his face and beat him with their fists, and some slapped him, **68** saying, "Prophesy to us, you Christ! Who hit you?"

Matthew 26:66-68

28 They stripped him and put a scarlet robe on him. **29** They braided a crown of thorns and put it on his head, and a reed in his right hand; and they kneeled down before him and mocked him, saying, "Hail, King of the Jews!" **30** They spat on him, and took the reed and struck him on the head. **31** When they had mocked him, they took the robe off him, and put his clothes on him, and led him away to crucify him.

Matthew 27:28-31

6 I gave my back to those who beat me, and my cheeks to those who plucked off the hair. I didn't hide my face from shame and spitting. **7** For the Lord GOD will help me. Therefore I have not been confounded. Therefore I have set my face like a flint, and I know that I won't be disappointed.

Isaiah 50:6-7

13 Behold, my servant will deal wisely. He will be exalted and lifted up, and will be very high. **14** Just as many were astonished at you—his appearance was marred more than any man, and his form more than the sons of men—

Isaiah 52:13-14

45 The sun was darkened, and the veil of the temple was torn in two. **46** Jesus, crying with a loud voice, said, "Father, into your hands I commit my spirit!" Having said this, he breathed his last.

Luke 23:45-46

5 They said to them, "Why do you seek the living among the dead? **6** He isn't here, but is risen."

Luke 24:5-6

25 He said to them, "Foolish men, and slow of heart to believe in all that the prophets have spoken! **26** Didn't the Christ have to suffer these things and to enter into his glory?"

Luke 24:25-26

8 And being found in human form, he humbled himself, becoming obedient to the point of death, yes, the death of the cross. **9** Therefore God also highly exalted him, and gave to him the name which is above every name . . .

Philippians 2:8-9

2 looking to Jesus, the author and perfecter of faith, who for the joy that was set before him endured the cross, despising its shame, and has sat down at the right hand of the throne of God.

Hebrews 12:2

4. We Have to Die to Go to Heaven

50 Now I say this, brothers, that flesh and blood can't inherit God's Kingdom; neither does the perishable inherit imperishable.

1 Corinthians 15:50

6 Therefore we are always confident and know that while we are at home in the body, we are absent from the Lord . . .

2 Corinthians 5:6

23 But I am hard pressed between the two, having the desire to depart and be with Christ, which is far better.

Philippians 1:23

8 We are courageous, I say, and are willing rather to be absent from the body and to be at home with the Lord.

2 Corinthians 5:8

21 For to me to live is Christ, and to die is gain.

Philippians 1:21

16 Therefore we don't faint, but though our outward person is decaying, yet our inward person is renewed day by day.

2 Corinthians 4:16

18 And the Lord will deliver me from every evil work, and will preserve me for his heavenly Kingdom. To him be the glory forever and ever. Amen.

2 Timothy 4:18

25 Jesus said to her, "I am the resurrection and the life. He who believes in me will still live, even if he dies."

John 11:25

11 This saying is trustworthy: "For if we died with him, we will also live with him. **12** If we endure, we will also reign with him."

2 Timothy 2:11-12

5. Death Is the Beginning of Heaven

23 But I am hard pressed between the two, having the desire to depart and be with Christ, which is far better.

Philippians 1:23

8 We are courageous, I say, and are willing rather to be absent from the body and to be at home with the Lord.

2 Corinthians 5:8

21 For to me to live is Christ, and to die is gain.

Philippians 1:21

43 Jesus said to him, "Assuredly I tell you, today you will be with me in Paradise."

Luke 23:43

6. We Will Be Resurrected into a New Body

50 Now I say this, brothers, that flesh and blood can't inherit God's Kingdom; neither does the perishable inherit imperishable.

1 Corinthians 15:50

22 For as in Adam all die, so also in Christ all will be made alive. **23** But each in his own order: Christ the first fruits, then those who are Christ's at his coming.

1 Corinthians 15:22–23

20 For our citizenship is in heaven, from where we also wait for a Savior, the Lord Jesus Christ, **21** who will change the body of our humiliation to be conformed to the body of his glory, according to the working by which he is able even to subject all things to himself.

Philippians 3:20-21

51 Behold, I tell you a mystery. We will not all sleep, but we will all be changed, **52** in a moment, in the twinkling of an eye, at the last trumpet. For the trumpet will sound and the dead will be raised incorruptible, and we will be changed. **53** For this perishable body must become imperishable, and this mortal must put on immortality.

1 Corinthians 15:51–53

54 But when this perishable body will have become imperishable, and this mortal will have put on immortality, then what is written will happen: "Death is swallowed up in victory." **55** "Death, where is your sting? Hades, where is your victory?" **56** The sting of death is sin, and the power of sin is the law. **57** But thanks be to God, who gives us the victory through our Lord Jesus Christ.

1 Corinthians 15:54–57

42 So also is the resurrection of the dead. The body is sown perishable; it is raised imperishable. **43** It is sown in dishonor; it is raised in glory. It is sown in weakness; it is raised in power. **44** It is sown a natural body; it is raised a spiritual body. There is a natural body and there is also a spiritual body.

1 Corinthians 15:42-44

2 Beloved, now we are children of God. It is not yet revealed what we will be; but we know that when he is revealed, we will be like him; for we will see him just as he is.

1 John 3:2

4 When Christ, our life, is revealed, then you will also be revealed with him in glory.

Colossians 3:4

36 For they can't die any more, for they are like the angels, and are children of God, being children of the resurrection.

Luke 20:36

3 Those who are wise will shine as the brightness of the expanse. Those who turn many to righteousness will shine as the stars forever and ever.

Daniel 12:3

43 Then the righteous will shine like the sun in the Kingdom of their Father.

Matthew 13:43

6. Live in Hope

1. Get the Eternal Hope

15 . . . The time is fulfilled, and God's Kingdom is at hand! Repent, and believe in the Good News.

Mark 1:15

30 "Sirs, what must I do to be saved?" **31** They said, "Believe in the Lord Jesus Christ, and you will be saved . . ."

Acts 16:30-31

9 . . . if you will confess with your mouth that Jesus is Lord, and believe in your heart that God raised him from the dead, you will be saved.

Romans 10:9

12 . . . for the same Lord is Lord of all, and is rich to all who call on him. **13** For, "Whoever will call on the name of the Lord will be saved."

Romans 10:12-13

18 He who believes in him is not judged.

John 3:18

24 Most certainly I tell you, he who hears my word and believes him who sent me has eternal life, and doesn't come into judgment, but has passed out of death into life.

John 5:24

9 By this God's love was revealed in us, that God has sent his one and only Son into the world that we might live through him.

1 John 4:9

23 For the wages of sin is death, but the free gift of God is eternal life in Christ Jesus our Lord.

Romans 6:23

2. Hope in God

18 For the needy shall not always be forgotten, nor the hope of the poor perish forever.

Psalm 9:18

18 Indeed surely there is a future hope, and your hope will not be cut off.

Proverbs 23:18

14 But I will always hope, and will add to all of your praise.

Psalm 71:14

20 . . . but rejoice that your names are written in heaven.

Luke 10:20

13 But, according to his promise, we look for new heavens and a new earth, in which righteousness dwells.

2 Peter 3:13

18 And the Lord will deliver me from every evil work, and will preserve me for his heavenly Kingdom. To him be the glory forever and ever. Amen.

2 Timothy 4:18

5 Why are you in despair, my soul? Why are you disturbed within me? Hope in God!

For I shall still praise him: my Saviour, my helper, and my God.

Psalm 43:5

18 Behold, the LORD's eye is on those who fear him, on those who hope in his loving kindness . . .

Psalm 33:18

5 Happy is he who has the God of Jacob for his help, whose hope is in the LORD, his God, **6** who made heaven and earth, the sea, and all that is in them; who keeps truth forever . . .

Psalm 146:5-6

25 For David says concerning him, "I saw the Lord always before my face, for he is on my right hand, that I should not be moved. **26** Therefore my heart was glad, and my tongue rejoiced. Moreover my flesh also will dwell in hope . . ."

Acts 2:25-26

7 . . . hope in the LORD, for there is loving kindness with the LORD. Abundant redemption is with him.

Psalm 130:7

11 This saying is trustworthy: "For if we died with him, we will also live with him. **12** If we endure, we will also reign with him."

2 Timothy 2:11-12

1 For we know that if the earthly house of our tent is dissolved, we have a building from God, a house not made with hands, eternal, in the heavens.

2 Corinthians 5:1

22 But you have come to Mount Zion, and to the city of the living God, the heavenly Jerusalem, and to innumerable multitudes of angels, **23** to the festal gathering and assembly of the firstborn who are enrolled in heaven . . .

Hebrews 12:22-23

13 But, according to his promise, we look for new heavens and a new earth, in which righteousness dwells.

2 Peter 3:13

23 Oh love the LORD, all you his saints! The LORD preserves the faithful, and fully recompenses him who behaves arrogantly. **24** Be strong, and let your heart take courage, all you who hope in the LORD.

Psalm 31:23-24

13 But now faith, hope, and love remain—these three. The greatest of these is love. **1** Follow after love . . .

1 Corinthians 13:13-14:1

3. Live by Faith

8 for by grace you have been saved through faith, and that not of yourselves; it is the gift of God . . .

Ephesians 2:8

1 Now faith is assurance of things hoped for, proof of things not seen.

Hebrews 11:1

24 For we were saved in hope, but hope that is seen is not hope. For who hopes for that which he sees? **25** But if we hope for that which we don't see, we wait for it with patience.

Romans 8:24-25

18 while we don't look at the things which are seen, but at the things which are not seen. For the things which are seen are temporal, but the things which are not seen are eternal.

2 Corinthians 4:18

7 for we walk by faith, not by sight.

2 Corinthians 5:7

17 But the righteous shall live by faith.

Romans 1:17

20 I have been crucified with Christ, and it is no longer I who live, but Christ lives in me. That life which I now live in the flesh, I live by faith in the Son of God, who loved me, and gave himself up for me.

Galatians 2:20

24 Those who belong to Christ have crucified the flesh with its passions and lusts.

Galatians 5:24

13 But now faith, hope, and love remain—these three. The greatest of these is love.

1 Corinthians 13:13

4. Live in Hope

20 . . . but rejoice that your names are written in heaven.

Luke 10:20

13 But, according to his promise, we look for new heavens and a new earth, in which righteousness dwells.

2 Peter 3:13

18 And the Lord will deliver me from every evil work, and will preserve me for his heavenly Kingdom. To him be the glory forever and ever. Amen.

2 Timothy 4:18

18 For the needy shall not always be forgotten, nor the hope of the poor perish forever.

Psalm 9:18

18 Indeed surely there is a future hope, and your hope will not be cut off.

Proverbs 23:18

14 But I will always hope, and will add to all of your praise.

Psalm 71:14

19 This hope we have as an anchor of the soul, a hope both sure and steadfast and entering into that which is within the veil . . .

Hebrews 6:19

24 Be strong, and let your heart take courage, all you who hope in the LORD.

Psalm 31:24

15 . . . Always be ready to give an answer to everyone who asks you a reason concerning the hope that is in you, with humility and fear . . .

1 Peter 3:15

23 let's hold fast the confession of our hope without wavering; for he who promised is faithful. **24** Let's consider how to provoke one another to love and good works, **25** not forsaking our own assembling together, as the custom of some is, but exhorting one another, and so much the more as you see the Day approaching.

Hebrews 10:23-25

13 But now faith, hope, and love remain—these three. The greatest of these is love.

1 Corinthians 13:13

5. Hoping in a Hopeless Situation

12 rejoicing in hope, enduring in troubles, continuing steadfastly in prayer . . .

Romans 12:12

5 and hope doesn't disappoint us, because God's love has been poured into our hearts through the Holy Spirit who was given to us.

Romans 5:5

25 For David says concerning him, "I saw the Lord always before my face, for he is on my right hand, that I should not be moved. **26** Therefore my heart was glad, and my tongue rejoiced. Moreover my flesh also will dwell in hope . . ."

Acts 2:25-26

21 This I recall to my mind; therefore I have hope. **22** It is because of the LORD's loving kindnesses that we are not consumed, because his mercies don't fail. **23** They are new every morning. Great is your faithfulness.

Lamentations 3:21-23

19 Remember my affliction and my misery, the wormwood and the bitterness. **20** My soul still remembers them, and is bowed down within me. **21** This I recall to my mind; therefore I have hope.

Lamentations 3:19-21

18 Against hope, Abraham in hope believed, to the end that he might become a father of many nations, according to that which had been spoken, "So will your offspring be."

Romans 4:18

19 Without being weakened in faith, he didn't consider his own body, already having been worn out, (he being about a hundred years old), and the deadness of Sarah's womb. **20** Yet, looking to the promise of God, he didn't waver through unbelief, but grew strong through faith, giving glory to God, **21** and being fully assured that what he had promised, he was also able to perform. **22** Therefore it also was "credited to him for righteousness."

Romans 4:19–22

19 God, your righteousness also reaches to the heavens. You have done great things. God, who is like you? **20** You, who have shown us many and bitter troubles, you will let me live. You will bring us up again from the depths of the earth.

Psalm 71:19-20

10 For you, God, have tested us. You have refined us, as silver is refined. **11** You brought us into prison. You laid a burden on our backs. **12** You allowed men to ride over our heads. We went through fire and through water, but you brought us to the place of abundance.

Psalm 66:10-12

9 as unknown, and yet well known; as dying, and behold, we live; as punished, and not killed; **10** as sorrowful, yet always rejoicing; as poor, yet making many rich; as having nothing, and yet possessing all things.

2 Corinthians 6:9-10

8 We are pressed on every side, yet not crushed; perplexed, yet not to despair; **9** pursued, yet not forsaken; struck down, yet not destroyed; **10** always carrying in the body the putting to death of the Lord

Jesus, that the life of Jesus may also be revealed in our body. **11** For we who live are always delivered to death for Jesus' sake, that the life also of Jesus may be revealed in our mortal flesh.

2 Corinthians 4:8-11

1 I waited patiently for the LORD. He turned to me, and heard my cry. **2** He brought me up also out of a horrible pit, out of the miry clay. He set my feet on a rock, and gave me a firm place to stand.

Psalm 40:1-2

5 Why are you in despair, my soul? Why are you disturbed within me? Hope in God! For I shall still praise him for the saving help of his presence.

Psalm 42:5

13 But now faith, hope, and love remain—these three. The greatest of these is love. **1** Follow after love . . .

1 Corinthians 13:13-14:1

6. Wait Patiently for God

5 Weeping may stay for the night, but joy comes in the morning.

Psalm 30:5

16 The LORD says: "Refrain your voice from weeping, and your eyes from tears, for your work will be rewarded," says the LORD.

Jeremiah 31:16

35 Therefore don't throw away your boldness, which has a great reward. **36** For you need endurance so that, having done the will of God, you may receive the promise.

Hebrews 10:35-36

12 rejoicing in hope, enduring in troubles, continuing steadfastly in prayer . . .

Romans 12:12

5 and hope doesn't disappoint us, because God's love has been poured into our hearts through the Holy Spirit who was given to us.

Romans 5:5

23 Oh love the LORD, all you his saints! The LORD preserves the faithful, and fully recompenses him who behaves arrogantly. **24** Be strong, and let your heart take courage, all you who hope in the LORD.

Psalm 31:23-24

21 This I recall to my mind; therefore I have hope. **22** It is because of the LORD's loving kindnesses that we are not consumed, because his mercies don't fail. **23** They are new every morning. Great is your faithfulness.

Lamentations 3:21-23

19 Remember my affliction and my misery, the wormwood and the bitterness. **20** My soul still remembers them, and is bowed down within me. **21** This I recall to my mind; therefore I have hope.

Lamentations 3:19-21

12 Blessed is a person who endures temptation, for when he has been approved, he will receive the crown of life which the Lord promised to those who love him.

James 1:12

11 Behold, we call them blessed who endured. You have heard of the perseverance of Job and have seen the Lord in the outcome, and how the Lord is full of compassion and mercy.

James 5:11

6 Wherein you greatly rejoice, though now for a little while, if need be, you have been grieved in various trials, **7** that the proof of your faith, which is more precious than gold that perishes even though it is tested by fire, may be found to result in praise, glory, and honor at the revelation of Jesus Christ . . .

1 Peter 1:6-7

11 "For I know the thoughts that I think towards you," says the LORD, "thoughts of peace, and not of evil, to give you hope and a future."

Jeremiah 29:11

5 Those who sow in tears will reap in joy. **6** He who goes out weeping, carrying seed for sowing, will certainly come again with joy, carrying his sheaves.

Psalm 126:5-6

25 The LORD is good to those who wait for him, to the soul who seeks him. **26** It is good that a man should hope and quietly wait for the salvation of the LORD.

Lamentations 3:25-26

18 Therefore the LORD will wait, that he may be gracious to you; and therefore he will be exalted, that he may have mercy on you, for the LORD is a God of justice. Blessed are all those who wait for him.

Isaiah 30:18

7. When Facing Death

1 The LORD is my shepherd; I shall lack nothing.

Psalm 23:1

10 Don't you be afraid, for I am with you. Don't be dismayed, for I am your God. I will strengthen you. Yes, I will help you. Yes, I will uphold you with the right hand of my righteousness.

Isaiah 41:10

4 Even though I walk through the valley of the shadow of death, I will fear no evil, for you are with me.

Psalm 23:4

5 I will in no way leave you, neither will I in any way forsake you.

Hebrews 13:5

20 Behold, I am with you always, even to the end of the age.

Matthew 28:20

5 Into your hand I commend my spirit. You redeem me, LORD, God of truth.

Psalm 31:5

59 They stoned Stephen as he called out, saying, "Lord Jesus, receive my spirit!" **60** He kneeled down, and cried with a loud voice, "Lord, don't hold this sin against them!" When he had said this, he fell asleep.

Acts 7:59-60

44 It was now about the sixth hour, and darkness came over the whole land until the ninth hour. **45** The sun was darkened, and the veil of the temple was torn in two. **46** Jesus, crying with a loud voice, said, "Father, into your hands I commit my spirit!" Having said this, he breathed his last.

Luke 23:44-46

43 Jesus said to him, "Assuredly I tell you, today you will be with me in Paradise."

Luke 23:43

8 For if we live, we live to the Lord. Or if we die, we die to the Lord. If therefore we live or die, we are the Lord's.

Romans 14:8

11 This saying is trustworthy: "For if we died with him, we will also live with him. **12** If we endure, we will also reign with him."

2 Timothy 2:11-12

14 For this God is our God forever and ever. He will be our guide even to death.

Psalm 48:14

23 Nevertheless, I am continually with you. You have held my right hand. **24** You will guide me with your counsel, and afterward receive me to glory.

Psalm 73:23-24

23 Are they servants of Christ? (I speak as one beside himself.) I am more so: in labors more abundantly, in prisons more abundantly, in stripes above measure, and in deaths often.

2 Corinthians 11:23

9 as unknown, and yet well known; as dying, and behold, we live; as punished, and not killed; **10** as sorrowful, yet always rejoicing; as poor, yet making many rich; as having nothing, and yet possessing all things.

2 Corinthians 6:9-10

8 We are pressed on every side, yet not crushed; perplexed, yet not to despair; **9** pursued, yet not forsaken; struck down, yet not destroyed; **10** always carrying in the body the putting to death of the Lord Jesus, that the life of Jesus may also be revealed in our body. **11** For we who live are always delivered to death for Jesus' sake, that the life also of Jesus may be revealed in our mortal flesh.

2 Corinthians 4:8-11

8 For we don't desire to have you uninformed, brothers, concerning our affliction which happened to us in Asia, that we were weighed down exceedingly, beyond our power, so much that we despaired even of life. **9** Yes, we ourselves have had the sentence of death within ourselves, that we should not trust in ourselves, but in God who raises the dead, **10** who delivered us out of so great a death, and does deliver; on whom we have set our hope that he will also still deliver us . . .

2 Corinthians 1:8-10

6 For I am already being offered, and the time of my departure has come. **7** I have fought the good fight. I have finished the course. I have kept the faith. **8** From now on, the crown of righteousness is stored up for me, which the Lord, the righteous judge, will give to me on that day; and not to me only, but also to all those who have loved his appearing.

2 Timothy 4:6–8

28 If you loved me, you would have rejoiced, because I said "I am going to my Father;" for the Father is greater than I.

John 14:28

13 I heard a voice from heaven saying, "Write, 'Blessed are the dead who die in the Lord from now on.'" "Yes," says the Spirit, "that they may rest from their labors; for their works follow with them."

Revelation 14:13

21 For to me to live is Christ, and to die is gain.

Philippians 1:21

23 But I am hard pressed between the two, having the desire to depart and be with Christ, which is far better.

Philippians 1:23

6 Therefore we are always confident and know that while we are at home in the body, we are absent from the Lord . . .

2 Corinthians 5:6

8 We are courageous, I say, and are willing rather to be absent from the body and to be at home with the Lord.

2 Corinthians 5:8

13 But now faith, hope, and love remain—these three. The greatest of these is love.
1 Follow after love . . .

1 Corinthians 13:13-14:1

7. What Will Remain Forever?

1. What You Did in God

12 Fight the good fight of faith.

1 Timothy 6:12

17 Whatever you do, in word or in deed, do all in the name of the Lord Jesus, giving thanks to God the Father, through him.

Colossians 3:17

31 Whether therefore you eat, or drink, or whatever you do, do all to the glory of God.

1 Corinthians 10:31

21 His lord said to him, "Well done, good and faithful servant. You have been faithful over a few things, I will set you over many things. Enter into the joy of your lord."

Matthew 25:21

16 Better is a little that the righteous has, than the abundance of many wicked.

Psalm 37:16

17 The world is passing away with its lusts, but he who does God's will remains forever.

1 John 2:17

2. What You Did for God's Glory

17 Whatever you do, in word or in deed, do all in the name of the Lord Jesus, giving thanks to God the Father, through him.

Colossians 3:17

31 Whether therefore you eat, or drink, or whatever you do, do all to the glory of God.

1 Corinthians 10:31

10 As each has received a gift, employ it in serving one another, as good managers of the grace of God in its various forms.

1 Peter 4:10

12 He said therefore, "A certain nobleman went into a far country to receive for himself a kingdom and to return. **13** He called ten servants of his and gave them ten mina coins, and told them, 'Conduct business until I come.'"

Luke 19:12-13

15 When he had come back again, having received the kingdom, he commanded these servants, to whom he had given the money, to be called to him, that he might know what they had gained by conducting business. **16** The first came before him, saying, "Lord, your mina has made ten more minas." **17** He said to him, "Well done, you good servant! Because you were found faithful with very little, you shall have authority over ten cities." **18** The second came, saying, "Your mina, Lord, has made five minas." **19** So he said to him, "And you are to be over five cities."

Luke 19:15–19

19 Don't lay up treasures for yourselves on the earth, where moth and rust consume, and where thieves break through and steal; **20** but lay up for yourselves treasures in heaven, where neither moth nor rust consume, and where thieves don't break through and steal; **21** for where your treasure is, there your heart will be also.

Matthew 6:19–21

3. Faith, Hope, and Love

3 If I give away all my goods to feed the poor, and if I give my body to be burned, but don't have love, it profits me nothing.

1 Corinthians 13:3

13 This is the end of the matter. All has been heard. Fear God and keep his commandments; for this is the whole duty of man.

Ecclesiastes 12:13

8 He has shown you, O man, what is good. What does the LORD require of you, but to act justly, to love mercy, and to walk humbly with your God?

Micah 6:8

23 This is his commandment, that we should believe in the name of his Son, Jesus Christ, and love one another, even as he commanded.

1 John 3:23

35 By this everyone will know that you are my disciples, if you have love for one another.

John 13:35

13 But now faith, hope, and love remain—these three. The greatest of these is love. **1** Follow after love . . .

1 Corinthians 13:13-14:1

8. How Can I Have That Lasting Hope?

1. Know That God Made You and Loves You

27 God created man in his own image. In God's image he created him; male and female he created them.

Genesis 1:27

13 For you formed my inmost being. You knit me together in my mother's womb.

Psalm 139:13

4 Since you have been precious and honoured in my sight, and I have loved you, therefore I will give people in your place, and nations instead of your life.

Isaiah 43:4

3 The LORD appeared of old to me, saying, "Yes, I have loved you with an everlasting love. Therefore I have drawn you with loving kindness."

Jeremiah 31:3

2. God Sent His Only Son Jesus to Save You

23 for all have sinned, and fall short of the glory of God . . .

Romans 3:23

27 Inasmuch as it is appointed for men to die once, and after this, judgment . . .

Hebrews 9:27

2 But your iniquities have separated you and your God, and your sins have hidden his face from you, so that he will not hear.

Isaiah 59:2

16 For God so loved the world, that he gave his one and only Son, that whoever believes in him should not perish, but have eternal life.

John 3:16

45 For the Son of Man also came not to be served, but to serve, and to give his life as a ransom for many.

Mark 10:45

5 But he was pierced for our transgressions. He was crushed for our iniquities. The punishment that brought our peace was on him; and by his wounds we are healed.

Isaiah 53:5

6 All we like sheep have gone astray. Everyone has turned to his own way; and the LORD has laid on him the iniquity of us all.

Isaiah 53:6

18 Because Christ also suffered for sins once, the righteous for the unrighteous, that he might bring you to God . . .

1 Peter 3:18

1 You were made alive when you were dead in transgressions and sins . . .

Ephesians 2:1

8 But God commends his own love toward us, in that while we were yet sinners, Christ died for us.

Romans 5:8

18 He who believes in him is not judged.

John 3:18

24 Most certainly I tell you, he who hears my word and believes him who sent me has eternal life, and doesn't come into judgment, but has passed out of death into life.

John 5:24

9 By this God's love was revealed in us, that God has sent his one and only Son into the world that we might live through him.

1 John 4:9

3. Accept God's Eternal Salvation through Faith

15 . . . The time is fulfilled, and God's Kingdom is at hand! Repent, and believe in the Good News.

Mark 1:15

30 "Sirs, what must I do to be saved?" **31** They said, "Believe in the Lord Jesus Christ, and you will be saved . . ."

Acts 16:30-31

9 . . . if you will confess with your mouth that Jesus is Lord, and believe in your heart that God raised him from the dead, you will be saved.

Romans 10:9

12 . . . for the same Lord is Lord of all, and is rich to all who call on him. **13** For, "Whoever will call on the name of the Lord will be saved."

Romans 10:12-13

15 Most certainly I tell you, whoever will not receive God's Kingdom like a little child, he will in no way enter into it.

Mark 10:15

3 Jesus answered him, "Most certainly, I tell you, unless one is born anew, he can't see God's Kingdom."

John 3:3

4. Leave Sin

9 Or don't you know that the unrighteous will not inherit God's Kingdom? Don't be deceived. . .

1 Corinthians 6:9

9 Whoever is born of God doesn't commit sin, because his seed remains in him, and he can't sin, because he is born of God.

1 John 3:9

29 If you know that he is righteous, you know that everyone who practices righteousness has been born of him.

1 John 2:29

24 Those who belong to Christ have crucified the flesh with its passions and lusts.

Galatians 5:24

20 I have been crucified with Christ, and it is no longer I who live, but Christ lives in me. That life which I now live in the flesh,

I live by faith in the Son of God, who loved me, and gave himself up for me.

Galatians 2:20

22 Many will tell me in that day, "Lord, Lord, didn't we prophesy in your name, in your name cast out demons, and in your name do many mighty works?" **23** Then I will tell them, "I never knew you. Depart from me, you who work iniquity."

Matthew 7:22-23

14 Blessed are those who do his commandments, that they may have the right to the tree of life, and may enter in by the gates into the city. **15** Outside are the dogs, the sorcerers, the sexually immoral, the murderers, the idolaters, and everyone who loves and practices falsehood.

Revelation 22:14–15

5. Live Right

18 We know that whoever is born of God doesn't sin, but he who was born of God keeps himself, and the evil one doesn't touch him.

1 John 5:18

13 This is the end of the matter. All has been heard. Fear God and keep his commandments; for this is the whole duty of man.

Ecclesiastes 12:13

8 He has shown you, O man, what is good. What does the LORD require of you, but to act justly, to love mercy, and to walk humbly with your God?

Micah 6:8

23 This is his commandment, that we should believe in the name of his Son, Jesus Christ, and love one another, even as he commanded. **24** He who keeps his commandments remains in him, and he in him.

1 John 3:23-24

16 We know and have believed the love which God has for us. God is love, and he who remains in love remains in God, and God remains in him.

1 John 4:16

14 Blessed are those who do his commandments, that they may have the right to the tree of life, and may enter in by the gates into the city. **15** Outside are the dogs, the sorcerers, the sexually immoral, the murderers, the idolaters, and everyone who loves and practices falsehood.

Revelation 22:14–15

21 Not everyone who says to me, "Lord, Lord," will enter into the Kingdom of Heaven, but he who does the will of my Father who is in heaven. **22** Many will tell me in that day, "Lord, Lord, didn't we prophesy in your name, in your name cast out demons, and in your name do many mighty works?" **23** Then I will tell them, "I never knew you. Depart from me, you who work iniquity."

Matthew 7:21-23

6 If a man doesn't remain in me, he is thrown out as a branch and is withered; and they gather them, throw them into the fire, and they are burned.

John 15:6

9 Even as the Father has loved me, I also have loved you. Remain in my love. **10** If you keep my commandments, you will remain in my love, even as I have kept my Father's commandments and remain in his love.

John 15:9–10

Printed in Great Britain
by Amazon

57217780R00099